MANAGING ADHD

WORKBOOK FOR WOMEN

MANAGING
ADHD

WORKBOOK
FOR WOMEN

Exercises and Strategies to Improve
Focus, Motivation, and Confidence

Christy Duan, MD
Kathleen Fentress Tripp, PMHNP-BC and
Beata Lewis, MD

ROCKRIDGE
PRESS

We dedicate this book to our patients, who are our best teachers. It is through their stories that we have learned the most. We strive to share lessons from their experiences with others so they can find healing and strength.

Interior and Cover Designer: Richard Tapp
Art Producer: Sara Feinstein
Editor: Laura Apperson
Production Editor: Caroline Flanagan
Production Manager: Holly Haydash

Art used under license from iStock. Author photos courtesy of Lea Cartier and Dalton Hernandez.

0 1 2 3 4 5 6 7 8 9 10

CONTENTS

———

INTRODUCTION

Welcome to *Managing ADHD Workbook for Women*! If you've picked up this book, you may be experiencing challenges with focus, organization, and efficiency. Everyone deals with difficulties like these from time to time, but people with ADHD struggle with these issues more often. The good news is that there are countless strategies and techniques that you can learn to manage these challenges and live a richer, more fulfilling life.

As mental health clinicians with decades of combined experience working with women who have ADHD, we have come to understand the unique challenges they face. You are not alone, and we've got you! We are excited to share our knowledge, and we feel honored to embark on this journey with you.

But before we get too ahead of ourselves, we'll give you a little introduction of who we are:

Hi! I'm Dr. Christy Duan, a psychiatrist based in New York City who treats children, adolescents, and adults. I also have specialized training in women's mental health, which includes issues around puberty, periods, pregnancy, and menopause. I really enjoy working with women who have ADHD. They are some of the most creative, daring, and energetic people I know.

I am Kathleen Fentress Tripp, a psychiatric nurse practitioner. I have worked for a decade with children and adults who struggle with a variety of mental health concerns and learning differences, including ADHD. I meet with kids and their families to evaluate, diagnose, and treat these concerns.

My name is Dr. Beata Lewis, founder of Mind Body Seven, a Brooklyn, New York, outpatient psychiatric practice. I am a child and adolescent psychiatrist who has been working with children and teens with ADHD since 2006. I experienced ADHD myself, especially when I was younger, and I figured out over time how to minimize the negative aspects of ADHD and leverage the positive aspect of hyperfocus in my own life (we'll talk about hyperfocus and how you can use it to your advantage as well).

We work together, and now we have written this book together, with the goal of creating a safe space for you to explore and embrace who you are, ADHD and all! This book is designed to help you understand how ADHD impacts you, reflect on yourself and your needs, find effective ways to work around your challenges, and celebrate your unique strengths.

HOW TO USE THIS WORKBOOK

Before we dive in, we'll explain how this workbook is organized so you can get the most value out of it. It is best for most women to work through the workbook in order, but feel free to adapt it to your unique style of learning. You may even choose to skim the book first or make a beeline to the section that is most exciting to you.

This workbook is divided into six chapters, which contain affirmations, patient stories, exercises, and key takeaways. Each chapter is designed to deepen your understanding of ADHD, help you appreciate the role of ADHD in your life, and learn valuable skills for managing ADHD symptoms. Please note that the affirmations in each chapter may not always feel like they apply to you. Feel free to adapt the affirmations so they are helpful for your unique situation.

Chapter 1 explains how ADHD affects women. You'll gain a better understanding of how ADHD plays a role in your work and commitments, family and relationships, time management, decision-making, and emotion regulation.

Chapter 2 presents research about underlying causes of ADHD, as well as how ADHD is diagnosed. You will learn about the three types of ADHD—inattentive, hyperactive/impulsive, and combined—and how the same diagnosis can look very different in two women. Finally, we'll do some myth-busting to help you differentiate between ADHD fact and fiction.

Chapter 3 introduces the concept of neurodiversity, which recognizes that people have neurological differences resulting in a wide range of strengths and weaknesses that are neither "good" nor "bad." Neurodivergence can be accommodated and celebrated rather than shunned; in fact, we'll explore how neurological diversity is essential to a healthy, thriving community. In this chapter, you'll learn how ADHD brings unique assets to your life that you can embrace and leverage.

Chapter 4 provides quick skill-building exercises that you can start using immediately. You'll learn and practice helpful strategies around procrastination, time management, organization, indecision, motivation, and emotional volatility or impulsivity. As you explore these skills, you will start building your own strategy tool kit that you can bring with you to any situation.

Chapter 5 takes you beyond self-reliance and explores how to ask for help and create a system of support to be your best self. Your network can include friends, family, and people in your workplace.

Chapter 6 discusses how you can determine whether it's time to seek professional help for your ADHD symptoms. We'll discuss therapy, medication, and lifestyle changes.

Although the exercises included in this workbook are designed to help you get started right away, this book is not intended to be a replacement for medical treatment. Chapter 6 has more information on seeking professional care. If you need more guidance on how to seek out care sooner rather than later, feel free to skip ahead to that final chapter.

A Note for Transgender and Gender-Diverse Women

Whether you are a cisgender, transgender, or gender-diverse woman, this book is meant for you. All women with ADHD face similar social and behavioral challenges, regardless of sex assigned at birth. This is because there has been a significant history of sexism and ableism that continues to affect women with ADHD to this day. These challenges can include navigating gender roles and expectations at home, school, and work, as well as socially.

Pushing past narrow definitions of how women should appear, think, feel, and behave is hard work! Fortunately, our society is shifting away from the denigration of people with disabilities and the myopic view of gender as binary (male or female), thanks to the radical work of disabled, neurodivergent, LGBTQIA+, and BIPOC groups, among others.

Furthermore, we know from research that ADHD is more prevalent in transgender and gender nonconforming people, when compared to cisgender people. Children with ADHD are more likely to identify as a different gender than their assigned sex than children without ADHD. The bottom line is this: Every person deserves a safe, supportive space to be seen, heard, and understood, and it is our hope that this book provides a welcoming space to all.

I'm a bright, intuitive, creative, passionate, and energetic person who happens to have ADHD. In fact, ADHD accentuates some of my best qualities. At the same time, I have unique challenges that I need to manage. Even when I struggle with getting distracted, I remind myself that the first step is to start. If I get distracted, I can always start again. Every moment is a new opportunity.

CHAPTER 1

The Effects of ADHD on Women

A s a woman with ADHD, you likely already have an intimate knowledge of how your symptoms affect you. In general, women with ADHD often face similar challenges, yet many feel that they are alone in their struggles. Women with ADHD frequently go undiagnosed, and even with a diagnosis, family, friends, and colleagues often misunderstand women's symptoms. If you have ever felt isolated in your experience, please know that you are not alone, and we will work together through this book to help you feel supported, understood, and empowered.

In this chapter, we'll present you with the most up-to-date information about the impacts of ADHD in women. You will learn ADHD subtypes and how ADHD differs by gender. Building on that groundwork, you'll have the chance to reflect on how ADHD shows up in your relationships with family, friends, and colleagues.

ADHD impacts executive functioning, which encompasses cognitive processes such as time management, decision-making, and more. If you've ever been overwhelmed with information that leads to decision paralysis and difficulty balancing short- and long-term goals, you're in good company—these kinds of issues affect many people with ADHD. You will learn how to make decisions that allow you to do the right thing at the right time, identify areas for improvement, and implement a short list of successful strategies to meet your goals.

Finally, we'll talk about emotion regulation, another core challenge for those with ADHD. This includes how you pay attention to, evaluate, and respond to various emotions. An exercise in this section will guide you on how you can accept and manage emotions more effectively.

Our hope is that you will be empowered by this knowledge and feel less isolated and more connected. By integrating our expert knowledge with your intimate knowledge of your symptoms, you can create a path to greater self-understanding, growth, and successful navigation of the different areas of your life.

JASMINE'S STORY

When Jasmine got a C in her college English class, she realized something was wrong. She had always excelled in high school. She was used to easily maintaining a solid A to B average. But this class required hours of reading, and she was unable to focus. She asked her professor for help. Her professor had struggled with ADHD in the past, too, and recognized that Jasmine had similar symptoms. She suggested that Jasmine seek out help from a doctor or mental health professional for her difficulties with focus. Jasmine was nervous about the psychiatry appointment she booked. She didn't know what to expect. After a thorough assessment, her psychiatrist diagnosed her with ADHD. She felt a sense of relief. She had always wondered what was "wrong" with her. The psychiatrist affirmed that there was nothing "wrong" with her. The psychiatrist explained that Jasmine's brain just worked a bit differently and that to succeed in college and beyond, it would greatly benefit her to learn some new strategies. When discussing treatment options, Jasmine felt a sense of hope that she had not experienced in a very long time.

The Unique Impacts of ADHD on Women

The path to an ADHD diagnosis can be a winding one for women. It is common for ADHD to go under-recognized in women, leaving them to struggle with challenging symptoms for years without understanding the cause or receiving the help needed.

In the United States, 6.1 million children have ADHD—this equates to 9.4 percent of all children in the country. There's a large discrepancy between the number of boys and girls diagnosed with ADHD; in fact, 12.9 percent of boys, compared to only 5.6 percent of girls, receive an ADHD diagnosis. In adults, studies estimate that the prevalence of ADHD is between 2.5 and 4.4 percent, with 5.4 percent of men having ADHD, compared to 3.2 percent of women.

This statistical difference between boys and girls stems from outdated biases about ADHD and gender. Because ADHD was previously thought to predominantly affect men, women received fewer diagnoses and were 3 to 16 times less likely to be referred for care. Additionally, clinicians and educators have a more difficult time recognizing ADHD symptoms in women. Women have more symptoms of inattention, which are harder to spot than those of impulsivity and hyperactivity. For example, a boy who leaves his seat or interrupts class is more likely to be identified to receive an ADHD diagnosis than a girl who quietly zones out. At the same time, women with hyperactive and impulsive symptoms are doubly impacted. These symptoms are more common in men, and they run contrary to society's stereotype of women being quiet, calm, and organized. These women face both the challenges of ADHD and social penalties for behaving outside the norm. To address this disparity, experts are collaborating to better identify and treat girls and women with ADHD.

There are three types of ADHD: inattentive, hyperactive/impulsive, and combined.

Those with **inattentive-type ADHD** often have difficulty paying attention to details, remaining focused, actively listening, following directions, remembering tasks, or organizing.

Symptoms such as fidgeting, restless behavior, interrupting conversations, and difficulty waiting for one's turn are signs of **hyperactive/impulsive-type ADHD**.

People with **combined-type ADHD** experience some degree of both sets of symptoms.

Next, we'll talk about the common challenges that affect women with ADHD in work and commitments, family and relationships, time management, decision-making, and emotion regulation. The accompanying exercises will help you to learn about and manage your ADHD symptoms in these areas.

Work & Commitments

ADHD can have a profound impact on work life and other important commitments. On the bright side, women with ADHD are known for their abilities to infuse creativity, dynamism, and "out-of-the-box" thinking into their work. In addition to these strengths, challenges in work may be present as well. These challenges will be unique to you, depending on your ADHD symptoms.

If you have inattentive-type ADHD, you may have to work harder or longer at accomplishing tasks that involve close attention to detail, sustained focus, and organization. Without the right accommodations to set you up for success, it's easy to overlook details and make simple mistakes. You might also get sidetracked and forget appointments or deadlines, assignments, and emails or calls needing your attention. In social contexts at work, it may take extra effort for you to focus during conversations and long meetings.

For women in high-pressure jobs with multiple responsibilities, focus can be even more difficult when many tasks need to be attended to throughout the day. If you are in a work environment like this, you may be at risk for burnout, a state of exhaustion where you feel less effective and more cynical about your work. When burnout leads to avoidance, you may feel reluctant to engage in tasks that require sustained attention or procrastinate to the point of missing deadlines.

Consider Riley, a patient with inattentive-type ADHD. They procrastinated on doing taxes every year because, as they put it, the attention and focus required seemed unmanageable and overwhelming. Riley decided to start a stimulant medication, which was helpful. Now, one month before taxes are due, they set themselves up for success by scheduling 30 minutes each morning to work on their taxes. They completed their taxes on time. This example illustrates how various strategies can work together to overcome procrastination.

Women with hyperactive-type ADHD have their own set of challenges. If you have hyperactive symptoms, you might feel a constant internal sense of restlessness that leads to difficulty sitting still for extended periods without fidgeting or talking. You might be best suited for workplaces that encourage movement, have an active and fast-paced atmosphere, and call for rapid decision-making.

Mercedes is a patient of ours who has hyperactive-type ADHD. She excelled as an assistant art director in NYC and was respected by her entire team. During meetings, Mercedes would often talk while someone else was talking. Her team members didn't see this as "interrupting," but rather as enthusiastic engagement in what was being discussed. Mercedes's team also valued her passion and quick, intuitive decision-making abilities.

When she was promoted to a new team based in the Midwest, her new teammates felt differently. During her annual review, she learned that coworkers felt "steamrolled" by her because they felt that she interrupted and dominated the conversation during meetings. Mercedes was upset by this and quickly excused herself after the review was done. She had the urge to slam the door shut and was later glad that she didn't. After simmering on it for a few days, she acknowledged that there was some truth to the feedback. Even though her style worked well for her in the past, it was not working for her now. Instead of remaining furious, Mercedes became curious about how ADHD was impacting her work relationships. She hired an executive function coach and worked through these challenges, retaining her strengths while tweaking other aspects of her behavior. At her next review, her boss praised the changes that she made.

How Does ADHD Show Up in Your Work and Commitments?

This exercise will help you target the work-related problems that impact you most. Rate the following items based on how you feel about their impact on your productivity by placing a check mark in the corresponding box.

	DOES NOT IMPACT ME AT ALL	IMPACTS ME A LITTLE	IMPACTS ME A LOT
I daydream at work.			
It takes me too long to finish tasks.			
I lose or misplace my purse, phone, laptop, chargers, or other work material.			
My body is restless at work.			
I get bogged down by hyperfocusing on one area of work while neglecting another.			
My work space looks messy and disorganized.			

	DOES NOT IMPACT ME AT ALL	IMPACTS ME A LITTLE	IMPACTS ME A LOT
I start projects but don't finish them.			
I interrupt during meetings.			
I struggle with deadlines because I underestimate how much time or effort they will take.			
I make careless mistakes.			
I reread emails because I miss important details on the first read.			
I procrastinate on responding to messages and doing work I find challenging.			

Take stock of the check marks you made under "impacts me a lot" and "impacts me a little." Consider the common threads among the issues you noted, and choose three problems that you'd like to focus on first. Keep these problems in mind as you work through this book and encounter strategies that may be effective to help with your ADHD symptoms at work.

Family & Relationships

In addition to work, ADHD can significantly impact family life and relationships. The effects of ADHD on relationships are not necessarily negative; in fact, they can bring out many positive attributes. Loved ones may feel energized around you and recognize that your sense of spontaneity and creative expression brings a lot of joy into their lives.

On the flip side, friends and family may complain about imbalanced relationships, issues with intimacy, and/or fraught dynamics. If you get easily sidetracked, you may be late to dates with friends and family (or completely forget to meet). You may forget to respond to emails, calls, and texts. Family and friends may take these behaviors personally. This can feel hurtful to you when you are trying your best with a brain that works differently from theirs. Of course, this does not have anything to do with how much you care for your loved ones, so communicating what you're going through and strengthening your organizational skills to respect important commitments can keep your treasured relationships humming along smoothly.

Dara is a patient who struggled with this exact issue. Her best friend, Ilana, was hurt and frustrated because Dara was often late to dates. Dara cared about Ilana deeply but had trouble managing her time and was frequently late. On the other end, Ilana had a history of conflict avoidance and was nervous about bringing up her feelings, yet she found the courage to do so because she valued their friendship. Ilana's honest approach gave Dara the opportunity to share her diagnosis of inattentive-type ADHD and reassure Ilana about how much she cared about their friendship. As a result, Ilana agreed to not take Dara's lateness personally, and Dara promised to keep better track of their plans with a detailed calendar. Once they made these changes, their friendship strengthened, and they each grew in important ways. Ilana could see that Dara wasn't flaky or careless—she just needed support to follow through on her commitments.

Hyperactive-type ADHD can interfere with relationships, because it leads to a constant sense of restlessness. As a response to this internal feeling, you may fidget, be talkative, or complete others' sentences. Many people aren't bothered by others' fidgeting and enjoy cooperative overlap during conversations. However, misunderstandings can impact your social relationships if other friends and family think you're impatient or not really listening.

If there is more than one person in an immediate family or group who has ADHD, communication can be more difficult due to challenges with inattention, restlessness, and impulsivity. This is a common occurrence, as the likelihood of inherited ADHD ranges from 70 to 80 percent in children and adults. That said, the strategies in this book can be used to help other members of your family, too.

Your ADHD Strengths and Challenges

ADHD can have both positive and negative impacts on your interpersonal life. To manage it effectively, it's important to identify the ways in which ADHD benefits you as well as the specific challenges you face because of ADHD.

Start off by listing five positive ways that ADHD impacts your family and relationships.

1. ....

2. ....

3. ....

4. ....

5. ....

Now list five negative ways that ADHD impacts your family and relationships.

1. ....

2. ....

3. ....

4. ....

5. ....

Now that you have an idea of how ADHD impacts your interpersonal life, both positively and negatively, you can appreciate the strengths it brings and use additional exercises in this book to manage its challenges.

Time Management

Research shows that individuals with ADHD have lower levels of dopamine and norepinephrine in parts of the brain. These neurotransmitters affect focus. Dopamine plays an important role in the reward system of the brain and impacts our attention, motivation, and pleasure. A simplistic way of thinking about it is that the more dopamine one has in certain parts of the brain, the more focus and motivation one can experience. People with ADHD have differences in dopamine regulation, leading to less focus on and interest in some activities.

This also affects time perception in ADHD. Time can be experienced in many ways, from the Earth's tilt that gives us the seasons to the phases of the moon. A neurotypical way of experiencing time is as a measurement of seconds, minutes, and hours. However, this is more difficult for people with ADHD. Because people with ADHD have a different internal clock, they can have difficulty with estimating how long things will take, or how much time has passed compared to neurotypical people's perceptions of time.

People with ADHD have an internal clock that can run faster, which is why boring tasks can seem like they drag on for much longer. For example, during the same hour-long work meeting, a neurotypical person could be easily engaged, while someone with ADHD could be bored and struggle to pay attention. The person with ADHD may need to take medication that regulates those neurotransmitters or do something daring and exciting—like starting a business—in order to get their dopamine and norepinephrine to an optimal level for attention, motivation, and pleasure. They also "feel" time in relation to rewards and emotions. When their neurotransmitter levels are optimized with rewards or emotionally stimulating situations, people with ADHD are able to keep track of time more like their neurotypical peers.

When you live in a world where your experience of time differs from most people's, you can encounter challenges in conventional time management. Being present in the here and now (as many people with ADHD are) is a good thing; it allows you to fully experience life in the moment. However, sometimes this presence can make executive functioning skills like planning, organizing, and self-regulating a bit more challenging.

You may not have difficulty doing a task well—the bigger problem is often making sure you complete the task on time. You might find that if you must complete an emotionally activating task right away, you can do it without a problem. Or you might prioritize doing something fun and easy now because it's more rewarding to do in the present. However, if you have a task with a faraway due date, you may find you procrastinate until you don't have enough time to do a good job. With ADHD, it can be harder to be motivated to accomplish a laborious, difficult task now, even if it reaps huge rewards in the future. This translates into difficulty balancing short-term and long-term goals.

One of our patients, Marguerite, noted that this was a major issue. She had an important 200-page report due in six months that could change the trajectory of her career. However, when she sat down to work, she couldn't help but notice dishes piling up in the sink and the dusty floors beneath her feet. Subsequently, she would always choose to wash dishes and sweep floors instead of writing her report. Marguerite enjoys tidying because the rewards are immediate. It's also hard for Marguerite to ignore the dishes and floors, which affect her in the present and are easier problems to solve, even if they're not that important.

As far as that huge report due in six months, Marguerite didn't see the point of doing it now. To complete the report, she would have to focus for long periods of time, something she had always found difficult. So even though it could mean a big promotion in the future, she found herself working on problems that brought more immediate, but less significant, rewards.

Scenarios like Marguerite's can present a conundrum. You might develop compensatory strategies, like overscheduling or overcommitting to things, so you can generate a sense of urgency to motivate yourself to complete tasks, but this can lead to burnout. To avoid the negative consequences of time mismanagement, it's important to identify the problems that result from your ADHD symptoms, such as procrastination, distraction, and disorganization. The following exercise can help you assess your time-management skills.

How's Your Time Management?

This exercise will help you determine how well you manage your time. Check the statements that are true for you.

☐ If I'm less than 15 minutes late, I consider myself on time.

☐ I often ask for extensions or return work after the due date.

☐ I hand in my work on time, but finish (and sometimes even start) at the last minute.

☐ I often stay up later than I'd like.

☐ Tasks usually take longer than I anticipate.

☐ I often can't finish timed tests.

☐ My friends know I'm usually late.

☐ I intend to get everything done, but usually run out of time.

☐ I need multiple reminders to leave so I can arrive on time.

☐ I procrastinate on tasks that I find most difficult.

If you checked more than three items, you probably struggle with time management. This is common in ADHD. The good news is, there are many strategies to help. For starters:

- Use a timer to keep yourself on track.

- Work on your most difficult tasks first, when your mind is fresh.

- Make a schedule and use your calendar every day.

- Use a to-do list and prioritize tasks.

  For more time-management strategies, skip ahead to page 58.

Decision-Making

Women with ADHD can find decision-making challenging. With so many decisions every day, anybody can get overwhelmed. In fact, a research study estimated that people make 200 food decisions each day. And that's just food—just imagine how many *other* decisions you make each day!

Sometimes women with ADHD can use their intuition to make great split-second decisions; other times, such impulsive decisions lead to regret. This can lead to excessive worrying about whether you are making the "right" decision. It could even lead to avoidance of making any decision at all, due to "wrong" decisions made in the past. Decision paralysis is an issue that comes up when you're bombarded by external stimuli and too many options. Consequently, you may flip-flop on issues and have difficulty coming to a decision.

Decision-making strategies are important because they help you streamline your day so you can feel relaxed and in charge. One key strategy involves learning how to prevent decision fatigue—the idea that the more decisions you make, the more difficult it is to make a good decision. After an exhausting day, you know you are experiencing decision fatigue when you can barely make up your mind about simple things, like what to eat for dinner. You might make a subpar decision, like eating a pint of chocolate ice cream for dinner instead of a well-balanced meal. Decision fatigue can happen to anybody—it's not exclusive to people with ADHD.

Several studies show that having too many decisions to make significantly reduces self-control. Lowered self-control can lead to procrastination, decreased persistence, and errors in judgment. Luckily, there are ways to prevent this.

To keep things simple, it's helpful to create boundaries around decision-making. This includes limiting your options. For instance, considering the pros and cons of two options before making a choice is less overwhelming than considering 50 options. Another limit is to schedule regular blocks of time for routine tasks so you don't have to decide about when to do them. That way, you have one fewer decision to make. In addition, focus on making a "good enough" decision, rather than a perfect decision.

To break free of indecision, you can slow the decision-making process by creating a visual breakdown of positive and negative consequences. The next exercise will help you assess how well you make decisions and develop strategies to make better ones.

Make a "Good Enough" Choice

In day-to-day life, we're all faced with some difficult decisions. A pro-con chart can help you identify which decision might be best for you. Think of a few tough choices you expect to face in the next few weeks. Choose one to fill out the following decision chart. List as many advantages and disadvantages as you can. Review the list to help you make the best choice for you in this situation. If there is another option, you can always re-create this chart on a separate piece of paper and add as many rows as you need.

		PROS	CONS
DECISION 1 **EXAMPLE:** *Cook a favorite meal at home with family.*			
DECISION 2 **EXAMPLE:** *Go out to dinner with friends instead.*			

Look carefully at the advantages and disadvantages you listed. Is Decision 1 or Decision 2 your best option in this situation? Which decision do you think you'll make?

Emotion Regulation

Emotions, which arise from situations in our daily lives, provide us with important information. Sometimes emotions come and go quickly. Other times, they linger for a long time. This depends in part on how we pay attention to the emotional situation, evaluate it, and respond to it.

Emotional dysregulation in women with ADHD can look like irritability, quickly changing moods, and emotions that are out of proportion to a given situation. Difficulties with emotion regulation can also come in the form of emotional outbursts, impulsive behavior, and aggression.

For some women, the emotional dysregulation that comes from ADHD can leave them feeling energized one moment and overwhelmed the next. They might act impulsively in order to feel good and energized again, or to avoid and move past feeling overwhelmed. It can be very difficult for some women with ADHD to sit with their emotions and tolerate situations that are unpleasant, because these women are remarkably sensitive to external stimuli. Compared with young adults without ADHD, young women with ADHD more frequently experience depression and suicidal ideation. Some women with ADHD are burdened by frequent irritability and anger that affects their ability to function in their work and relationships. Depression and associated irritability and anger are treatable. If you experience depression, irritability, or suicidal ideation, please reach out to a psychotherapist, psychiatrist, or another healthcare professional for help. See the Resources (page 121) for website links to find a professional in your area. Chapter 6 (page 97) provides more guidance on seeking out professional help.

When it comes to hormone-related mood disorders, studies suggest that women with ADHD are more likely to have premenstrual dysphoric disorder and postpartum depression and anxiety than the general population.

Women with ADHD may spend a lot of time "sensation-seeking"—that is, looking for ways to experience intense feelings and excitement. This can include taking physical, social, financial, and legal risks for the sake of the experience. Although some sensation-seeking can cause problems, there are many safe ways to seek adventures and new experiences.

The following exercise will help you understand different ways of regulating emotions and explore how and when to use these different styles.

What's Your Emotional Management Style?

This exercise is based on Stanford psychologist James Gross's five-step model of emotion regulation. Under each of the five different emotional management styles listed here, you'll find an example. Use this example to help you write about a situation from your life in which you used that strategy. Notice if there are strategies here that you would like to incorporate in your life.

STEP 1: CHOOSE YOUR SITUATION.
Example: To avoid interacting with a difficult coworker after a long week, Brigitte chose to go home and relax instead of going to happy hour.
Your example:

....

....

STEP 2: CHANGE YOUR SITUATION.
Example: Beth hates public speaking but had to give a long presentation. To make the situation better, she included comic strips and made jokes that her audience liked.
Your example:

....

....

STEP 3: SHIFT YOUR ATTENTION.
Example: Shasta was nervous about attending a karaoke night that their ex was attending. They decided to focus on the karaoke singers instead of their ex.
Your example:

....

....

STEP 4: REFRAME THE SITUATION AND YOUR ABILITIES.

Example: Nekeyia was anxious about a big project. She reminded herself that she had done a successful job on similar projects, and that there was no project that was "too big"—everything could be broken down into smaller pieces.

Your example:

....

....

....

STEP 5: CHANGE YOUR RESPONSE.

Example: Emily felt offended by a friend's statement. Instead of reacting immediately like she had in the past, she reminded herself of the value of their relationship before choosing to respond.

Your example:

....

....

....

Which strategies do you use most frequently?

....

....

....

CHEN'S STORY

Chen is a botanist with ADHD. She has always been curious about how her sense of time differs from that of other people. She has difficulty completing some tasks on time but can do other tasks quickly and easily. For instance, Chen takes three times as long to write research grants as the other botanists and often arrives late to meetings. She finds grant writing and meetings tedious and boring, but she can easily spend hours learning about moss and can quickly make insightful connections about different moss species. When Chen began reading more about how people with ADHD experience time, she felt validated. Of course she "feels" time! Her internal clock runs on emotion. The stronger the emotion that's generated by the people and activities involved, the timelier she is. Simply put, the more rewarding the activity, the easier it is for her to accomplish the task. Chen also discovered that ADHD medications helped her with time management and productivity, as did listening to music while grant writing.

Key Takeaways

In this chapter, we explored the unique impacts of ADHD on women. From research, we know that men are twice as likely to be diagnosed with ADHD as women. Because ADHD is under-recognized in women, there are misunderstandings about what might be contributing to their difficulties in life. Once a woman understands her ADHD, there are many things she can do to take control of her symptoms.

ADHD causes difficulties in executive functioning, which can include planning, organizing, and regulating emotions. These difficulties may appear in work and commitments, family and relationships, time management, decision-making, and emotion regulation.

Identifying ADHD allows women to address symptoms and achieve greater self-understanding and self-compassion. ADHD treatments such as medication, therapy, lifestyle modifications and behavioral strategies can make a big difference in how you feel, perceive yourself, interact with your friends and family, perform at work, and function in the world.

As we wrap up this chapter, consider these action steps that you can use going forward:

- Reflect on how ADHD symptoms affect you in a positive way.

- Recognize how ADHD shows up in your work and commitments by reflecting on any difficulties you have in the workplace.

- Consider how ADHD shows up in your relationships and any changes you'd like to make to improve your relationships.

- Time management is not an issue of laziness but of planning and organization. Don't be too hard on yourself! Use strategies that work for you (page 58).

- Identify areas in your life where you feel decision paralysis (page 13). Think about ways that you can break decisions into smaller parts, limit options, focus on making a "good enough" choice, or place a time limit on decisions.

- Reflect on how you manage your emotions and consider changes you can make in the future.

Just because my brain works differently from other people's does not mean there is something "wrong" with me. My brain is beautiful and works in a way that is unique to me. Sometimes the way my brain works creates challenges for me. That's okay—I am up for the challenge! I know that identifying these challenges and learning how to manage them more effectively can allow me to enjoy a richer, more fulfilling life.

Knowledge is power. My ADHD diagnosis can set me free and is the key to knowing how to help myself. By understanding the challenges that accompany ADHD, I can take steps to best care for myself. I am committed to meeting my full potential. Understanding ADHD allows me to understand my needs better. I am grateful for this opportunity to know myself.

CHAPTER 2

Understanding ADHD

This chapter is full of keys that can help you unlock a deeper understanding of your ADHD.

The first key is to get insight from the information available. The *Diagnostic and Statistical Manual of Mental Disorders, Fifth Edition (DSM-5)* is used by clinicians to diagnose ADHD. Although ADHD begins in childhood, there are plenty of adults affected by ADHD. We'll explore what the research shows about underlying causes of ADHD, such as brain chemistry and structural differences, and how it can run in the family.

The second key is to recognize the many faces of ADHD. Because there are three types of ADHD—inattentive, hyperactive/impulsive, and combined—it may seem that individuals would fit into these clear-cut categories. But there's more to it, because each woman with ADHD is unique, has distinct gifts and challenges, and will experience ADHD differently.

The third key is to separate fact from fiction. There are many misconceptions about ADHD, and we'll help debunk the most common myths.

The fourth and final key is to take the adult ADHD self-assessment exercise developed by the World Health Organization. In under five minutes, you'll be able to identify your ADHD symptoms, giving you a road map for discussing it with medical professionals.

By the end of this chapter, we hope you'll give yourself a pat on the back and say, "Achievement unlocked!"

ANA'S STORY

Ana was diagnosed with ADHD at the age of 66. When she was a child, ADHD wasn't a diagnosis. It wasn't until the late 1960s, when Ana was in her teens, that the American Psychiatric Association formally recognized ADHD as a condition. As a child, Ana often got in trouble for talking out of turn, getting up out of her seat, and failing to pay attention. She always thought her restlessness was just anxiety. Ana wondered why she wasn't like everyone else. Why did she always feel restless and anxious? Why did she have memory trouble? This led to a lifetime struggle with depression and anxiety.

Once she received her ADHD diagnosis, the pieces of the puzzle fell into place. She read a couple of books on the subject, started working with a life coach, and began taking ADHD medications that improved her symptoms. In addition to helping her focus and get things done, the medication relieved her long-standing feelings of anxiety and restlessness. For the first time in her life, she felt like she understood and even loved herself. Her self-esteem issues melted away, and her vivacious, energetic personality finally shone through.

What Is Adult ADHD?

ADHD is a pattern of inattention, hyperactivity-impulsivity, or both. When these patterns negatively impact social, academic, or occupational activities, it is diagnosable as ADHD. A diagnosis can be established by a computerized test, neuropsychological testing, or clinical assessment.

The American Psychiatric Association bases the diagnosis of ADHD on the following symptoms:

INATTENTIVE-TYPE ADHD SYMPTOMS	HYPERACTIVE/IMPULSIVE-TYPE ADHD SYMPTOMS
Inattentiveness to detail or a tendency to make careless mistakes	Fidgeting or squirming
Difficulty focusing on activities	Inability to sit still
Difficulty listening when directly spoken to	Restlessness or inappropriate movement in certain situations
Difficulty following instructions and finishing tasks	Difficulty engaging in quiet activities
Difficulty organizing activities	Feeling as if "on the go" or "driven by a motor"
Avoidance of activities requiring sustained attention	Excessive talkativeness
Difficulty keeping track of items	Difficulty waiting their turn in conversations
Tendency to be easily distracted	Difficulty waiting for their turn
Forgetfulness about daily tasks	Tendency to intrude on others' activities or conversations

To receive a diagnosis for the inattentive and hyperactive/impulsive ADHD types, six or more symptoms from that category must be present for at least six months in two or more settings (such as home, school, work, interpersonal relationships, etc.). For combined-type ADHD, six or more symptoms must be present from each category. These symptoms must also be present in at least two settings for over six months.

ADHD begins in childhood. To receive a diagnosis of any type of ADHD, several symptoms must be present before age 12. It can be difficult for adults to recall their childhood ADHD symptoms accurately, so it can be helpful for clinicians to receive information from patients' parents. If that's not an option, input about current symptoms from a partner, close friend, or coworker can also help clinicians diagnose ADHD.

You might wonder where ADHD symptoms come from. Certain genes are correlated with ADHD, but the exact cause is unknown. Most experts believe that there are many contributing factors. We know from research that ADHD has a genetic component. The likelihood that you and an immediate biological relative (parents, siblings, or children) both have ADHD is high—the heritability is about 74 percent.

Research has shown differences between the brains of people with and without ADHD. For example, people with ADHD tend to have lower brain volumes, areas in the brain that mature more slowly, differences in connections between parts of the brain, and different levels of the neurotransmitters dopamine and norepinephrine, compared with people without ADHD. We know these differences are present, but we are not sure whether they cause ADHD. It's important to note, however, that none of this has any bearing on intelligence. People with ADHD are just as smart as people without ADHD.

The Many Faces of ADHD

If you've seen one person with ADHD, then you've seen only one person with ADHD. There are as many different experiences of ADHD as there are people! Everyone is wired differently, and people are diverse in their personalities, experiences, upbringings, and lifestyles. Two women who have the same diagnosis may have different symptoms.

Amanda and Zadie both have combined-type ADHD. This means they have both inattentive and hyperactive-impulsive symptoms. In childhood, Amanda was full of energy—her teacher called her the "Energizer Bunny"—and she had trouble sitting still. Zadie was known as a restless daydreamer in school, because she would fidget in her seat, lose focus, and sometimes forget her homework.

In this case, Amanda struggled more with hyperactive-impulsive symptoms, and Zadie struggled more with inattentive symptoms. Some kids loved Amanda because of her bubbly nature, and others disliked her because she interrupted them. Amanda's parents had faced similar challenges and grew out of them as teens, so they weren't concerned about Amanda's behaviors. Zadie was generally liked by the other kids because she was less impulsive. Instead, she made careless errors on quizzes and had organizational difficulties. At home, she struggled with emotion regulation, which concerned her parents. She overcame most of these challenges with the support of her parents and teachers and the use of a planner.

Amanda struggled more with her symptoms over time, and Zadie's symptoms improved with organizational strategies. Amanda didn't "grow out" of her ADHD symptoms like her parents expected—in fact, 75 percent of those diagnosed with ADHD in childhood continue to experience symptoms into adulthood. As her academic difficulties worsened in high school, her self-esteem plummeted. She began skipping classes and turned to alcohol to cope. Conversely, Zadie learned strategies to manage her symptoms and excelled in high school.

Amanda's parents became worried and arranged for her to see a psychiatrist. After a thorough evaluation, she received a diagnosis of ADHD. Zadie did not receive an ADHD diagnosis until she saw a psychiatrist at her university, where she had more difficulty keeping up.

Amanda's psychiatrist recommended medication, which she was initially hesitant about. But because she was struggling so much, she decided to give it a try. She tried several medications before finding the one that worked best for her. Amanda's emotion regulation, attention, and hyperactivity-impulsivity improved. She stopped self-medicating with alcohol. As she started thriving academically, she gained self-confidence and completed her studies to become an elementary school teacher. Now in her work with children, she keeps an eye out for kids with symptoms like hers and supports them and their families in pursuing the right care.

Zadie's psychiatrist offered her ADHD medication and explained the risks, benefits, and alternatives to treatment. Even though she decided not to start medication, the ADHD diagnosis helped her make sense of her experience. She sought therapy to improve her executive functioning, doubled down on strategies to manage symptoms, and was able to enter her dream PhD program.

Starting medication and therapy is a personal decision that's best discussed with a mental health professional who specializes in ADHD. Sharing your values and priorities with a mental health professional is helpful, because they will be able to answer your questions accurately and walk you through the pros and cons regarding medication. That way, you can be fully informed and make the best decision for you.

Key Takeaways

We hope you now have a better understanding of how ADHD is diagnosed. The stories of Amanda and Zadie illustrate how two women with the same diagnosis can have very different life experiences. Here are some key points to keep in mind:

1. ADHD is a long-standing pattern of inattention and/or hyperactivity-impulsivity that begins before age 12 and affects development and functioning in more than one setting, including home, school, work, interpersonal relationships, or other activities.

2. ADHD is a clinical diagnosis made based on symptoms listed in the *DSM-5* and is divided into three subtypes: inattentive-type ADHD, hyperactive-/impulsive-type ADHD, and combined-type ADHD.

3. ADHD is highly heritable.

4. The neurotransmitters dopamine and norepinephrine play a role in ADHD.

5. Research shows consistent differences between the brains of people with ADHD and neurotypical people, yet we do not fully understand how these differences lead to ADHD.

Just because I have an ADHD diagnosis doesn't mean that my ADHD looks the same as another person's ADHD. The gifts and challenges of each person's ADHD manifest in unique ways. The solutions to those challenges can be just as different, and I am learning what works best for me.

Fact vs. Fiction: Debunking Common ADHD Myths

Incorrect information about ADHD abounds. In addition, ADHD symptoms are often missed and misinterpreted by educators, family members, and even clinicians. Here is a list of common ADHD myths that we'll debunk for you.

MYTH: People with ADHD aren't as smart as people without ADHD.

FACT: People with ADHD can be just as smart as people without ADHD. A range of IQs exist in the general population and among people with ADHD. Someone with a genius-level IQ can have ADHD. ADHD just means that your brain works differently from other people's brains. The brain chemicals and pathways that control attention, focus, impulse control, planning, and reward simply work differently in people with ADHD than in those without ADHD.

MYTH: People with ADHD are always moving around and talking.

FACT: This is not always true. Indeed, some people with ADHD have hyperactive and impulsive symptoms. However, others have inattentive-type ADHD that leads to difficulties with focus and organization. Because inattentive-type symptoms tend to be less noticeable and disruptive, they are easy to miss. People with inattentive symptoms often get diagnosed later in life than those with hyperactive or impulsive symptoms.

MYTH: If I've been diagnosed with ADHD, I'll struggle at school and work.

FACT: Many people with ADHD excel at school and work, and others struggle. However, with lifestyle modifications and treatment, those who have struggled with their academics and career can make a big turnaround and be successful. We've worked with many patients with ADHD who used to dread school or work ADHD is treatable, and ADHD symptoms can fade into the background with the right treatment plan, including work and life adjustments, and in some cases, therapy and medications. By following a treatment plan, people with ADHD can reach their full potential.

MYTH: If someone has always gotten good grades, they don't have ADHD.

FACT: Straight-A students can have ADHD, although they may not be diagnosed as quickly as those who struggle. Some people with high IQs or highly developed coping strategies can make it through high school or college without their ADHD impacting their grades. Some patients are not diagnosed with ADHD until the demands on their attention became exceptional, such as in graduate school or a high-intensity job. During such high-demand periods, the coping mechanisms of adults with undiagnosed ADHD may break down, and ADHD symptoms may suddenly become more apparent. This is one reason why some people are not diagnosed with ADHD until adulthood.

MYTH: Girls and women don't have hyperactive ADHD.

FACT: Studies show that girls and women with ADHD do have hyperactive and impulsive symptoms, but they are typically less obvious than those of boys and men. For instance, boys and men tend to have more behavior problems such as not following rules, disrespecting the rights of others, and behaving in socially inappropriate ways. Girls and women tend to display more social-relational problems, such as blurting out hurtful comments when angered, self-harming, or engaging in impulsive sexual behaviors.

ADHD Self-Assessment

The World Health Organization Adult ADHD Self-Report Scale (Resources, page 121) can help you determine if you have symptoms of adult ADHD and which symptoms affect you the most. You can find the eighteen-question ADHD Self-Report Scale online by searching for "The World Health Organization Adult ADHD Self-Report Scale" or "ASRS Screener." There are three websites listed in Resources (page 121) where you can find the full assessment.

Once you're ready to take the assessment, rate yourself on the questions based on the last six months by marking an X in the box that describes your experience. Part A includes the six questions that are most predictive of symptoms consistent with an ADHD diagnosis. Part B includes twelve other helpful questions.

When you've completed the assessment, you can determine your score. Your symptoms are highly consistent with an ADHD diagnosis if you have four or more marks in the "sometimes," "often," and/or "very often" boxes in Part A. For Part B, additional marks in the "sometimes," "often," and/or "very often" boxes suggest that ADHD could be having an impact on you.

Write down your score below. How did you feel while taking this assessment?

_____

_____

_____

_____

_____

_____

_____

Use the next two pages to journal about your experience taking the assessment and to reflect on what you've learned so far.

Which question(s) in Part A did you identify with most strongly? Why?

_____

_____

_____

_____

_____

_____

_____

_____

_____

Review your answers in Part B and reflect on how ADHD could be having an impact on you.

_____

_____

_____

_____

_____

_____

_____

_____

_____

Compare your answers with the chart of symptoms for inattentive and hyperactive/impulsive ADHD types (page 23). Which symptoms do you experience? Did you learn anything new about yourself after taking this assessment?

_____

_____

_____

_____

_____

_____

_____

_____

_____

_____

_____

_____

_____

_____

_____

_____

THE IMPORTANCE OF AN OFFICIAL DIAGNOSIS

The World Health Organization Adult ADHD Self-Report Scale is a useful tool for screening ADHD symptoms; however, it's not a replacement for a formal diagnosis from a medical professional. Think of this questionnaire as a starting point—from here, you can more deeply explore your symptoms and share your questionnaire results with the medical professional you are working with.

To give a formal diagnosis of ADHD, a clinician may ask about your symptoms in childhood, because they show up in different ways in adulthood. Also, medical professionals may have to pay especially close attention to ADHD symptoms in women, because symptoms are more subtle in women than in men. Furthermore, women with ADHD may be better than men at developing coping strategies that mask their symptoms. To do a thorough assessment, the professional would need to ask if you have a history of inattention, academic difficulties, emotional reactivity, anxiety, depression, poor self-esteem, risky behavior, challenges with peer relationships, and/or physical complaints.

Being a strong advocate for yourself may sometimes be important in getting help for your ADHD. If you ever feel your symptoms are being dismissed, it's okay to be clear and direct. You could say, "I would like to be evaluated for ADHD" or "please refer me for an ADHD evaluation," if you feel your healthcare professional is not taking your concerns seriously.

It's important to receive a thorough diagnostic evaluation for ADHD, because symptoms can persist and have a tremendous impact on your career, relationships, and even safety. To begin this process, ask for referrals from your primary care doctor or insurance carrier, or browse through the *Psychology Today* or Good Therapy website (see Resources, page 121).

I know that ADHD can be subtle, because women are more likely to have inattentive symptoms than men. I'm glad that I can forge a path forward now that I have insight into how ADHD affects women and how it uniquely affects me. I am understanding myself more every day.

Key Takeaways

After reading this chapter, we hope you have a clearer understanding of ADHD and how it affects you. ADHD can have a major impact on school, work, and social life. Unfortunately, the diagnosis is often delayed in women because girls and women present more often with inattentive symptoms that are often missed. As a result, women may experience anxiety, depression, low self-esteem, substance abuse, and other problems. A formal diagnosis requires working with a clinician who will assess your symptoms, though hopefully the World Health Organization Adult ADHD Self-Report Scale gave you some idea of where you stand.

Here are some action steps in the meantime:

- Reflect on Ana's story from page 22. Use the following write-in lines to consider how your symptoms might impact your mood, anxiety level, and self-esteem.

  - Mood: ....

    ....

  - Anxiety level: ....

    ....

  - Self-esteem: ....

    ....

- Review the *DSM-5* criteria (page 23) and consider what symptoms you currently face in the inattentive and hyperactive/impulsive categories. Remember that these symptoms must be present for at least six months in two or more settings and affect you negatively.

  - Do you have at least six symptoms in the inattentive category? YES / NO

  - Do you have at least six symptoms in the hyperactive/impulsive category? YES / NO

  - Do you have at least six symptoms in both categories? YES / NO

- Do these symptoms impact you negatively? YES / NO

- In what settings do these symptoms arise? ....

  ....

  ....

- Think back to your childhood, before you were 12 years old, and consider what symptoms (page 23) you dealt with back then.

  - What symptoms were present?

    ....

    ....

    ....

    ....

    ....

    ....

- Ask your parents, siblings, other family members, partners, close friends, and trusted coworkers about how they see ADHD impacting different areas of your life.

  - What did they share?

    ....

    ....

    ....

    ....

    ....

    ....

- If you haven't already completed the World Health Organization Adult ADHD Self-Report Scale, do so now and take it to your next appointment with a medical professional.

We all have brains that work differently. My neurodivergence benefits who I am, both in my work and my personal life. There is nothing wrong with thinking, feeling, or acting differently from other people. We should be ourselves! We all have our own unique abilities and challenges, regardless of ADHD, and I embrace mine.

CHAPTER 3

Embracing Your Neurodivergence

The natural world is filled with beauty, diversity, and wonder. During his 1830s voyage, scientist and explorer Charles Darwin admired the remarkable assortment of birds in the Galápagos Islands and how they adapted to many environments. Some finches wielded pointed beaks to expertly tweeze worms from the ground. Other finches employed their broad beaks to efficiently crush the hulls of seeds. Darwin understood how biodiversity is a key indicator of health in an ecosystem.

Australian sociologist Judy Singer developed a similar understanding of how neurological diversity is a key indicator of health in the human species. Singer coined the word *neurodiversity* in her 1998 honors thesis, which spurred a new paradigm of understanding in the social justice and disability rights movements.

As someone who identifies as "being in the middle of three generations of women 'somewhere on the autistic spectrum,'" Singer understood first-hand how people who think differently face oppression, just as others are oppressed based on race, gender, sexuality, and socioeconomic class. This can include people with autism spectrum disorder, ADHD, learning differences, intellectual differences, depression, anxiety, and much more.

Singer shifted our understanding from a medical perspective, which focuses on causes and cures of a "disorder," to a sociological perspective that recognizes that people may have neurological differences that result in strengths and weaknesses. These qualities only become disabilities if society rejects those differences and fails to provide accommodations that allow people to live to their fullest potential. This viewpoint celebrates neurological differences as essential and inseparable parts of one's identity that are not inherently "good" or "bad."

In this chapter, you'll learn how to embrace your neurodiversity. This means that you don't need to change who you are. Instead, you can learn how to be *more* yourself by celebrating your brain's uniqueness. By learning strategies that tap into your strengths and use your unique gifts to your advantage, you can redefine success. You are wonderful exactly as you are! We are all on a lifelong journey to enhance our ability to be with our emotions and bodies and develop the skills to lead a meaningful life in integrity with our values.

PADMI'S STORY

Padmi is a customer service representative and mother of three children, and she has ADHD. When she's not working, she loves socializing with friends, zipping around the city on her moped, and spending time outdoors with her wife and kids. For a long time, Padmi didn't know how to make her ADHD work for her. In middle school, Padmi would be the first to finish her work. Feeling bored, she would chat with other kids and distract them from their work. Teachers were frustrated by this, but they recognized that she was gifted. They gave Padmi additional work and the freedom to choose what she wanted to learn in her extra time. Now at work, Padmi's quirks are a big asset. She is known as an excellent communicator who applies her hyperfocus to problem-solving for customers. She's called on to make smart, intuitive decisions while dividing her attention between several urgent issues at a time. At home, Padmi asks her wife to catch her eye when she's telling her something important so she knows to pay close attention. Padmi brings a lot of excitement into their shared life by finding activities and adding them to their online calendar. Her wife makes sure they are prepared and on time.

Working With, Not Against, Your Mind

When you embrace your neurodivergence, you let go of being "like everyone else." This frees up energy for you to figure out how to tap into your unique assets. You may need to advocate for yourself at school, at work, and in relationships in order to receive the accommodations you need to reach your full potential—Padmi's story shows these accommodations in action. When you take responsibility for your actions and work hard in a supportive environment, the sky's the limit.

As a woman with ADHD, you may have been called "quirky" throughout your life. Some women cope with this by masking their ADHD symptoms to fit in with neurotypical society or to conform to gender roles. Instead of changing to fit someone else's idea of "normal," you can shift your focus to embrace your neurological blueprint. Your mind is unique to you, and there is no such thing as a "good" or "bad" brain.

How your specific qualities of attention and behavior are viewed depends on the context. What might be a strength in one situation could be a weakness in another. Interrupting a conversation among friends to chime in will be perceived differently than interrupting your boss. As our society progresses in the view of neurodiversity as an asset, we realize that what was once a weakness can be considered a strength.

Following is a list of eight common strengths of people with ADHD. As you go through this section, think about how you embody each of these traits.

1. **AUTHENTIC:** Although some women with ADHD mask their symptoms to fit in, many simply cannot. If this resonates with you, you may have developed an identity as a neurodivergent "outsider." And being outside the norm can be a wonderful place to be! People may view you as authentic, charming, interesting, and refreshing.

2. **CREATIVE:** Because women with ADHD are neurodivergent, they've had to develop unconventional ways to succeed. If you're creative, you may tend to exhibit "out-of-the-box" thinking, grasp the "bigger picture" quickly, and link seemingly unrelated ideas to create new understandings.

3. **DARING:** Women with ADHD may be more comfortable taking risks. When others don't like this quality, they may call you "impulsive." Yet when it works well, you may be called "daring," "spontaneous," and "courageous." By taking calculated risks, women with ADHD can reap big rewards and revel in the thrill of it. Women

with ADHD are often good at navigating uncertainty, and that's advantageous in many circumstances.

4. **ENERGETIC:** Women with hyperactive ADHD traits can be known as energetic doers, leaders, and initiators. Energetic women can bring a spark to a room and exude confidence. Well-managed energy can help you inspire others, innovate, and perform at a high level.

5. **HYPERFOCUSED:** Women with ADHD can focus for long periods on subjects of interest. This intensity and passion can lead to success and expertise in a given area. Many women with ADHD recognize hyperfocus as a positive trait that enhances productivity and the ability to become a topic expert.

6. **INQUISITIVE:** Many women with ADHD have lively minds that are easy to engage and inspire. These ambitious explorers are open to new experiences and hungry for knowledge. If you're inquisitive, you may be great at hands-on learning and getting out there to discover things for yourself.

7. **PERCEPTIVE:** Although women with ADHD can sometimes be called "inattentive," they are often so receptive to stimuli that it can be overwhelming. You may perceive a lot during any given interaction and can make quick, intuitive decisions. For some, this can translate to performing well under the pressure of a deadline or a crisis.

8. **RESILIENT:** Because most women with ADHD are used to navigating a society that does not accommodate their neurodivergence, they tend to develop resiliency and the ability to adapt to various situations. Maybe you've had to work twice as hard in school or work. It takes grit and perseverance to keep bouncing back and remaining engaged in a society that is only beginning to accept neurodiversity.

Key Takeaways

All people—whether they have ADHD or not—have unique gifts and challenges. But because many women with ADHD live in a society that labels ADHD symptoms as impediments, it's necessary to reframe this negative programming and embrace the positive qualities that ADHD brings.

Women with ADHD may need to find settings, activities, and types of work that fit them well. For some, working from home can help. For others, working in a place with lots of stimulation and deadlines is best. You may find that you're more likely to succeed in fields where you can use your specific ADHD strengths.

By developing a deep understanding of your unique neurological blueprint and using it to serve you, you can work with—not against—your own mind.

Before moving on to the next section, reflect on these questions:

1. What are advantages, or strengths, of your ADHD?

    ....

    ....

    ....

    ....

    ....

2. What are disadvantages, or weaknesses, of your ADHD?

    ....

    ....

    ....

    ....

    ....

3. Describe a situation in which your ADHD helped you reach a goal.

_____

_____

_____

_____

_____

_____

_____

4. Describe a situation in which your ADHD made it more difficult for you to reach a goal.

_____

_____

_____

_____

_____

_____

_____

5. What would you miss if your ADHD went away?

_____

_____

_____

_____

_____

As a woman with ADHD, I'm wired differently from neurotypical people. It's great that many people are suited to a typical 9-to-5 job. And it's perfectly fine that I'm not. I work well in flexible, high-pressure settings where I can use my hyperfocus to dive deep into topics that interest me and use my creativity to solve complex problems. My ADHD allows me to experience and contribute to the world in a unique way.

CAMILLE'S STORY

Camille is a graphic artist with ADHD. Though she eventually found success at an advertising firm, she first had to overcome many obstacles. She went to a liberal arts college after high school but disliked some of her classes and struggled to pass. Even though she dropped out of college for a while, she never lost sight of her goal to become an artist. Her parents called her "headstrong" and "stubborn." They wanted her to settle down in a stable, steady career instead of taking a risk on a design job. Camille preferred to look at herself as "determined" and "tenacious." She transferred to an art school that provided accommodations and the support of an organizational tutor. After graduating, Camille sent her portfolio to all the major advertising firms in the country and faced a slew of rejections for two years. But she had a lot of grit. She took their feedback, refined her work, and finally landed a position at a great agency. Despite her difficulties with sitting still and focusing, her talent for visual metaphor and close attention to detail made her stand out. Though she lacked patience, her impulsivity gave her a reputation for being a quick self-starter who took initiative. Camille used her creative mind to improve existing designs and experiment with innovative approaches that advanced her field.

Learning to Embrace Your Quirks

Neurotypical society has a narrow definition of how women should think, feel, and behave. For many women with ADHD, it's difficult to fit in, and their "quirks," or ADHD symptoms, significantly impact their lives. You might feel like you're walking on a tightrope and worry that you're bound to fall at some point. But what if there's a way to step off the tightrope? What if, instead of falling, you can fly?

If you've ever had the sense that you're "too much" or "not enough," we hope that you'll come away knowing that you're never too much and you're always enough. You don't need to hide your most authentic self to be accepted and find success. You can use your eccentricities to your advantage, instead of quashing them. Here are three examples of powerful women with ADHD who have learned how to embrace their quirks:

Simone Biles

Gymnast Simone Biles has won 32 Olympic and World Championship medals, making her one of the most decorated gymnasts in history. In 2016, hackers exposed her confidential medical records with the intention of revealing an "unfair advantage" because she used ADHD medication. In her response, Simone's quirks of authenticity and fearlessness shone through, just as they do in her Olympic performances. She said that she has ADHD and that there's nothing shameful about using appropriate medical treatments. The Olympic authorities confirmed that she was approved to use the medication, which put her on a level playing field with other competitors.

Lisa Ling

Lisa Ling is a journalist, television personality, and author who was diagnosed with inattentive-type ADHD at the age of 40 while she was reporting on it! Lisa had long suspected that there was something different about her because of her focusing quirks. She remembered going through entire classes without retaining any information if she wasn't interested in the subject. At the same time, she credits this quirk with her success: "As a journalist, when I'm immersed in a story, then I feel like I can laser-focus. But if I'm not working, my mind goes in every direction but where it's supposed to go."

Karina Smirnoff

Karina Smirnoff is one of the featured dancers on the hit reality show *Dancing with the Stars*. She is also a choreographer, fitness teacher, and fashion designer. A friend saw how Karina's quirks impacted her life and encouraged her to see a doctor. In an interview, Karina said that she coped with her hyperactive quirks by getting involved with figure skating, ballet, gymnastics, and piano from a young age. As an adult, she manages her symptoms with medication and strategies such as taking frequent breaks during her 10-hour rehearsals.

You Don't Have to Do Things Like Everyone Else

Being "successful" can mean different things and be achieved in different ways. For many women, mastering the hyperfocus of their ADHD can result in a kind of a super-power, allowing them to get a lot of high-quality work done quickly. For others, the ability to jump between various tasks and come up with creative solutions on the fly is integral to their personal and professional achievements.

Many of our patients use ADHD traits to their advantage and don't try to fit themselves into neurotypical molds. For example, rather than trying to slog through a 9-to-5 work schedule, Gina thrives by breaking her workday into smaller chunks over a 12-hour period and taking breaks in between. Charelle maximized her potential when she was flexible in the way she ordered the steps of a task, sometimes doing step 7 before step 3, for example.

Laurie Dupar, founder of her own coaching business, has publicly shared in an article in *ADDitude* magazine that she sees her ADHD brain as a huge asset and com-ponent of her success: "Running your own business and being an entrepreneur requires the ability to manage chaos, unpredictability, and inconsistency. People with ADHD, with their high interest and tolerance for the new and stimulating, are often at their best in what would be a crisis situation for someone else. In fact, these are the exact situations when they tend to be most focused and clear-headed. We eat chaos for breakfast."

Everyone should allow themselves to work in the ways that work for them, guilt-free, knowing that this is one of the best ways to optimize their functioning. "Your way" might include multitasking, taking frequent breaks, using a fidget gadget, listening to music, doing your work at a certain time of day, or any other trick you've discovered.

The following exercise will help you identify your ADHD-related cognitive strengths and find ways to let them shine.

Getting the Job Done, Your Way

Think about the unique way your brain works. Then write down some nontraditional approaches you take to get your jobs done. Use the example to help guide your journaling. Next to each approach, come up with a way this has helped you or could help you in the future.

Example: Multitasking—As a store manager, juggling more than one project at a time engages my mind and keeps work fresh and interesting.

1. ....
....
....
....
....

2. ....
....
....
....
....

3. ....
....
....
....
....

Each day, I make the decision to choose myself. Instead of squashing my quirks, I embrace them and strive to live the most authentic life possible. I can use my quirks to my advantage, first by understanding myself and what works for me. Strategies that work for neurotypical people may not be the best for me, and I don't have to do things like everyone else. I can accomplish my goals in my own way and define success for myself.

Key Takeaways

We hope this chapter provided you with a greater appreciation for your neurodivergence and how to work with authenticity. As you move on to the next chapter, consider these key takeaways:

1. Just as biodiversity is a key indicator of health in an ecosystem, neurodiversity is a key indicator of health in the human species. Neurological differences are essential and inseparable parts of one's identity, and there is no "good" or "bad" difference.

2. The focus on "normalizing" neurodivergent people is oppressive. Instead, we can build a win-win society by accepting neurodiversity and focusing on how to offer environments in which all people, including those with ADHD, can thrive.

3. By understanding and embracing your neurological blueprint, you can learn how to work with—not against—your own mind.

4. Women with ADHD have many positive qualities and quirks. Women with ADHD may be seen as authentic, creative, daring, energetic, hyperfocused, inquisitive, perceptive, and resilient.

5. What works for some people may not work for you. Don't be afraid to do things differently. Remember that you are resilient and can try new approaches to define your own success.

I will embrace the ways in which ADHD makes me stronger and use strategies to cope with the ways it challenges me. I'm developing skills and strategies that make me more effective in my personal and professional life. Everyone has strengths and challenges. I can use my skills and strategies to get through any challenge.

CHAPTER 4

Strategies You Can Start With

Get ready to get empowered! This chapter will provide you with skills that address common struggles faced by women with ADHD. If you've ever dealt with issues managing procrastination, time management, organization, indecision, motivation, emotion regulation, or impulsivity, this chapter can be used to build your own tool kit of strategies. These skills are designed to improve functioning by freeing you from ineffective patterns of behavior, presenting workarounds for getting things done, and demonstrating effective management of relationships. Even though we have created these tips and exercises specifically for women with ADHD, they can be helpful to any woman struggling in these areas. If you find something that works for you, feel free to share it with a friend!

When Geri wanted to get pregnant, she had to decide whether to stop taking the ADHD medication that she had been on since she was 10. It was a difficult decision because her medication—methylphenidate—really quieted her feelings of restlessness, a troublesome symptom of her combined-type ADHD. After talking with her psychiatrist about the risks and benefits of staying on methylphenidate during pregnancy, Geri made the decision to stop methylphenidate prior to trying to conceive. Though Geri was initially nervous to stop a medicine that had helped her manage her ADHD for many years, she decided to take the leap and work with her therapist on behavioral strategies to manage her restlessness, distractibility, and poor time management. Though she had difficulties at first, the behavioral strategies she learned worked surprisingly well. Geri used strategies such as list-making, breaking work into chunks, taking movement breaks, and using a timer to help her body stay calm and her mind focused. Geri plans to stay off medication until she is done breastfeeding, when she'll work with her therapist to determine next steps.

Your Strategy Tool Kit

This section will provide strategies to build your tool kit of skills. Each set of skills is followed by an exercise to practice the new skills and strategies. The more you practice skills for the ADHD symptoms that bother you most, the more easily you will be able to access them when you need them.

Throughout this chapter, we will introduce 21 skills that address common symptoms of ADHD. If the skills apply to your unique situation, add them to your tool kit. If not, feel free to personalize them to make them work for you. As you read about the different strategies, think of ways you can apply them to your everyday life. This might involve remembering times when they would have been helpful and anticipating times when they might work well in the future.

The areas we will focus on in this section are avoiding procrastination, managing time well, getting organized, feeling confident in your decisions, feeling motivated, regulating strong emotions, and decreasing impulsive behavior. The goal is to build your confidence and success in managing the symptoms that challenge you most.

For Procrastination

It can be difficult to start an uninteresting yet important task that requires a lot of concentration and focus. But avoiding these tasks may result in a pileup of work that feels overwhelming. Here are four strategies—three to minimize procrastination and one to work with it:

1. **MAKE A TO-DO LIST.** When you make a to-do list, your brain doesn't have to work so hard to keep track of it all. It can also feel great to cross things off your list.

2. **BREAK TASKS INTO SMALL CHUNKS.** Large tasks can feel overwhelming and make it hard to get started. Breaking a big task into smaller bits can feel more manageable and approachable.

3. **USE A BODY DOUBLE.** If you've tried using the first two strategies and are still struggling, try using a body double. Using a body double means being in the same physical space as someone who is doing what you are aiming to do. For example, if you're working on a complex project at work, it may be helpful to work in the same space as a coworker who is also working, such as in a conference room. If you are having trouble tackling household chores such as cleaning, try doing this at the same time as your roommate or partner. Having a body double helps keep you on track and accountable.

4. **SCHEDULE CATCH-UP TIME.** Designate a time in your calendar to work on the things that you tend to avoid. Ideally, this would be a time when your brain and concentration are at their best, such as morning for early birds or evening for night owls. This could be a recurring block of time in your calendar on a selected day of the week. You can use this time for catching up on tedious tasks, administrative tasks, or anything else you tend to avoid. This strategy is geared toward working with procrastination by creating time to specifically work on those annoying tasks you've put off.

Don't Delay, Bust Procrastination Now

In this exercise, you'll test out the various strategies you just learned to see which works best for getting a job done. Keep in mind that some strategies may work better than others depending on the task.

1. Write down one household task that you must do every week, like shopping for groceries or doing the laundry.

   ....

   ....

2. On a scale from 1 to 10, with 10 being most confident, how confident do you feel about completing this task?

   (1) (2) (3) (4) (5) (6) (7) (8) (9) (10)

3. To discover which task management strategies might work best for you for this task, try a new one each week:

   - In week 1, place the task on a to-do list and check it off when it's complete. Then reflect on the results. Did creating a to-do list help you more easily complete the task?

   ....

   ....

   ....

- In week 2, break the task down into three or more smaller steps. Then reflect on the results.

  ....

  ....

  ....

- In week 3, ask someone to be your body double. Then reflect on the results.

  ....

  ....

  ....

- In week 4, allot a specific time on your calendar to do the task. Then reflect on the results.

  ....

  ....

  ....

4. Which strategy worked best for you? Which one was least helpful? Do you think there might be a different strategy that would work even better?

  ....

  ....

  ....

  ....

For Time Management

Many adults struggle with time management, but people with ADHD have a distinct challenge in this area. Research has shown that having ADHD can change your perception of time. Here are two tips for improving time management:

1. **MAKE A REALISTIC SCHEDULE.** First, identify times when a schedule can be useful, such as morning or evening routines or workday periods. When do you struggle most to manage time? This is the perfect place to try implementing a schedule to help keep you on track. You'll need to specify the things you need to get done during a given time, as well as estimate the amount of time each task will take. For example, if you are working on a morning schedule to get out the door on time, you may estimate that it will take 10 minutes to brush your teeth and get dressed. If it ends up taking 20 minutes, you can revise your schedule. Feel free to revise the schedule until it works for you.

2. **USE A TIMER.** Using a timer is an effective strategy for getting lots done in a specific period. For example, if you are sifting through unread emails, set a timer for 15 to 20 minutes during which you are completely dedicated to this task. By leaving other distractions for later, you can be surprisingly productive in a short time. You can also use a timer to stay focused on your schedule in strategy 1.

In the following exercise, you'll make a morning schedule to get out the door on time.

Make a Morning Schedule

List everything you need to do between waking up and leaving home. Then estimate how long each task takes. The first line is filled in for you as an example.

MORNING TASKS	TIME
Brush teeth and wash face	*5 minutes*
TOTAL TIME	

Look at the total time of your morning tasks. Now add a 10-minute buffer as extra insurance against any unforeseen delays. What is the total now?

Based on the number of minutes you wrote in the chart, figure out how much time you will need each morning to get ready to leave the house on time.

Try using a timer to keep you on schedule with each task. As you practice your morning routine, make adjustments as needed. If you need encouragement to get out of bed on time, include something that you enjoy right at the beginning of your morning routine, such as taking a shower, drinking a cup of coffee, or listening to music or podcasts.

Also, feel free to use the same strategy at other times of day or in situations where you struggle to manage your time.

For Disorganization

Keeping things organized, orderly, and tidy will make your day and life run more smoothly. When things are well organized, you're less likely to lose or forget things. ADHD can make staying organized difficult, which can make your physical and mental spaces feel chaotic. Here are some useful strategies to help with disorganization:

1. **USE CHECKLISTS.** Checklists are a concrete way to stay organized. For example, in operating rooms and scientific procedures, checklists are often used to be sure nothing is missed. You can apply this strategy for times when you get disorganized. For example, making a checklist of key items to bring to work can prevent you from forgetting essential items. Checklists can be used for a one-time occasion, such as planning a special event, or on a repeated basis, such as a morning checklist.

2. **PRACTICE DECLUTTERING.** Are you drowning in "stuff"? Having fewer things makes it easier to keep a space tidy and organized. Decluttering includes getting rid of or donating items and clothes you no longer use and discarding trash to clear your space. Emotional attachment can make it hard to get rid of certain items. Try these tips to make parting with things easier:

   - Ask yourself, "Have I used this item in the last year?" If not, it's probably a good time to let it go.

   - Ask yourself, "When is the next time I will use this item?" If you can't think of an immediate need, this may be a good item to let go of.

   - Donate the things you no longer need. Then you'll know that someone else will get to enjoy them. This feels better than throwing things away and reduces waste.

   - Picture your space organized and free of clutter. This vision can be inspiring!

3. **KEEP IT SIMPLE.** Sometimes our best efforts to organize can be too much of a good thing. For people who are naturally very organized, using a multitiered, color-coded system may work well, but we recommend a simpler approach for people with ADHD. For example, instead of trying to organize bills such as by date or vendor, simply keep one folder for bills that you address each week or month. Another example is using a bin for things like hats and gloves, instead of trying to organize by folding or hanging, which may be so much work that you end up not putting them away at all. Think of how to set up your organizational system into a "one-step" process—for example, drop the clothes into an open-top hamper, place mail in a designated bin, etc.

Get Your Bag in Order

Think about a bag you carry often. Do you have trouble keeping it organized? Our client Johanna was often running late in the morning because she had to go back home to look for her phone or something else she had forgotten. We worked with Johanna to create a bag checklist, which helped her keep organized. For her, the key items were her phone, charger, wallet, keys, and asthma inhaler.

Create your own bag checklist. Having your actual bag beside you for reference may help as you work on this exercise.

☐ .... ☐ ....

☐ .... ☐ ....

☐ .... ☐ ....

☐ .... ☐ ....

☐ .... ☐ ....

Now copy this list onto a separate page and post it at home near your bag.

One more tip: Keeping an organized bag isn't just about remembering to put everything in—it can also involve taking things out! If your bag is cluttered with things that aren't necessary, consider removing them to keep things tidy.

For Indecision

Indecision is paralyzing and gets in the way of moving forward. Many capable women have shared that they have trouble making and sticking to their decisions. If you can relate to this issue, you may get so preoccupied with trying to make the best decision that it becomes hard to make any decision at all. Here are some ways to combat indecision:

1. **USE A PRO-CON LIST** (see page 14 or page 63). A pro-con list allows you to outline and compare the positive and negatives of various decisions.

2. **CONSIDER BOTH SHORT- AND LONG-TERM OUTCOMES.** Sometimes one decision will feel very appealing in the short term, but not so appealing when long-term consequences are considered. The opposite can also be true. Balancing short- and long-term outcomes is a key consideration in good decision-making.

3. **REJECT PERFECTIONISM.** Don't let perfectionism paralyze you. Remember that there are probably many good decisions, rather than just one perfect decision. This more flexible mindset reduces indecision and getting stuck. Ask yourself, "If I'm not making an active choice, what choice am I making?" Oftentimes, lack of decision-making is a decision in and of itself.

4. **TAKE AN OUTSIDE PERSPECTIVE.** When you're struggling to make a decision, sometimes viewing things from a different perspective can provide valuable insight. What advice would you give a friend or family member faced with the same decision?

Pro-Con List for Decision-Making

Think of a choice you have to make in the next week and come up with at least two possible decisions you could make. Then develop a pro-con list to help you decide.

What's the choice you have to make?

_____

_____

_____

POSSIBLE DECISION 1:

_____

_____

_____

List the pros of this decision:

_____

_____

_____

List the cons of this decision:

_____

_____

_____

What are the immediate outcomes of this decision?

_____

_____

_____

CONTINUED >

What are the long-term consequences of this decision?

....

....

POSSIBLE DECISION 2:

....

....

List the pros of this decision:

....

....

List the cons of this decision:

....

....

What are the immediate outcomes of this decision?

....

....

What are the long-term consequences of this decision?

....

....

What decision will you make? What made you choose this one?

....

....

For Motivation

Our motivation is what drives us and inspires us to achieve our goals. We need motivation to achieve big goals, as well as more routine goals such as completing chores or taking care of ourselves and others. ADHD can make it challenging to stay motivated, particularly for difficult, tedious, or detail-oriented tasks. Figuring out what motivates you can help keep you focused and on task, even when it's a difficult job. Remembering your motivations can also help you get back on track when you hit a bump in the road. Here are some strategies to build and maintain motivation:

1. **UNDERSTAND THE MOTIVATION BEHIND YOUR GOALS.** Clearly defining your goals and what inspires them can help you maintain motivation. Try making a visual representation of these, such as on sticky notes or a visual dream board with photos. For example, if you have a goal of keeping a tidy home but find yourself struggling to get motivated to clean, it may be helpful to create a note reminding yourself of your motivation. For example, the note could read, "I feel centered when my space is organized."

2. **VISUALIZE ACHIEVING YOUR GOAL.** Imagining what will happen if you achieve your goals can be inspiring and motivating. Athletes who need to motivate themselves to train often visualize themselves scoring a goal or winning a race. This strategy can work for many types of tasks. For example, if you have a goal of completing one job application a day but find it difficult to feel motivated, visualizing yourself working at a new job may help inspire you.

3. **USE INCENTIVES.** Rewarding yourself for goal-oriented behavior can boost motivation. For example, a woman who has a goal of becoming physically fit but struggles to find the motivation to exercise may benefit from rewarding herself when she does exercise. One woman we know, Cat, rewards herself for getting on the treadmill by watching one of her favorite reality shows as she exercises.

Build Motivation

The following exercise will help you identify some of your goals and what inspires them. When setting goals, it is ideal to follow the SMART goal-setting format—that is, setting goals that are specific, measurable, achievable, relevant, and time-bound. This chart will help you do just that. The first column is filled out for you as an example.

EXAMPLE	YOUR GOAL #1	YOUR GOAL #2
GOAL: Attend three exercise classes in the next seven days.	GOAL:	GOAL:
I WANT TO ACHIEVE THIS GOAL BECAUSE: *I believe this is the path to achieving better physical health.*	I WANT TO ACHIEVE THIS GOAL BECAUSE:	I WANT TO ACHIEVE THIS GOAL BECAUSE:
IF I ACHIEVED THIS GOAL: *I would feel proud as well as physically healthy and would be setting a great example for my kids.*	IF I ACHIEVED THIS GOAL:	IF I ACHIEVED THIS GOAL:

Naming your goals and the reasons you want to achieve them is like mapping your motivation. If you lose your way, you can come back to this exercise to get on track. Your goals may change over time, so update your list of goals for the year, month, or week regularly to stay on track.

For Emotion Regulation

Strong, positive emotions, such as falling in love or excitement about a fun experience, feel wonderful. However, sometimes emotions become so strong that they are difficult to manage. When we are feeling emotionally dysregulated, or "off," we may say and do things that aren't in our best interest or that we later regret. This type of impulsivity is not unique to ADHD. In fact, most people tend to be more impulsive when faced with overwhelmingly strong emotions. Here are a few strategies for managing strong emotions and impulsivity:

1. **STOP IN YOUR TRACKS.** Just that—don't do anything. The emotional center of our brain works much faster than the logical part. When we are highly emotional, sometimes we make split-second decisions that bypass the logical part of our brains entirely. By taking a pause, you can give yourself time to think things through so you don't act impulsively.

2. **NAME YOUR EMOTION.** It may sound strange, but bringing what you are feeling to your conscious awareness by labeling it is a first step in regulating your emotions. Ask yourself, "What am I feeling right now?" It could be joy, anger, fear, disappointment, or disgust—whatever it is, label it. If you are having a difficult time with labeling, describing the bodily sensation first can help you identify the emotion.

3. **CALM YOUR BODY.** When we are in a highly emotional state, our body changes. We may experience changes in heart rate, blood pressure, muscle tension, and pain sensations. Calming techniques you can do in the moment include paced breathing, applying cold water to your face, progressive muscle relaxation (tensing then relaxing one part of your body at a time), and other relaxation and mindfulness techniques that can help steady your nervous system and your body.

Regulate Your Emotions

Think of a recent time when you felt overwhelmed, irritated, or acted impulsively in reaction to your emotions. Can you picture how you felt in that situation? What emotion do you feel now as you hold this image in your mind's eye?

....

What physical sensations are you feeling in your body now as you think back to that situation?

....

....

On a scale of 1 to 10 (10 being the most intense), what is the intensity of your emotion?

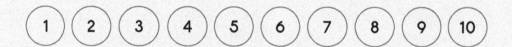

Now, for three minutes, practice slow breathing. Take a regular inhale and then extend your exhale to at least twice as long as the inhale. If extending the breath is difficult, try pretending that you are breathing through a straw. That should slow your breathing so that your exhale is longer than your usual inhale.

What is the intensity of your emotion now?

For Impulsivity

Our brains automatically work to achieve an optimal level of stimulation. For neuro-typical brains, usual day-to-day stimulation can be enough. Therefore, a neurotypical person may have no problem paying attention to a speaker. ADHD brains may need higher levels of stimulation. A woman with ADHD may have a lot of difficulty paying attention to the same speaker, but feel "right" taking a risk. This can include actions like starting a company, traveling spontaneously, driving very fast, skydiving, training for a marathon, gambling, buying items, arguing, making jokes, and more. Although people may call people with ADHD "impulsive," they might also be described as "daring," "spontaneous," and "courageous" when risk-taking is managed well. If speaking or acting impulsively has ever been problematic for you, these strategies may help:

1. **PRESS PAUSE!** Knowing when to pause before speaking or acting can serve you well. There are times when acting quickly can work in your favor and others when it won't. Think about the kinds of situations in which it is most useful to pause and think ahead of time—this premeditation can help you know to press the pause button when necessary.

2. **GO SLOW.** If you create more distance between your urges and subsequent actions, this can help you manage your impulses effectively. Slowing things down and taking time to consider your next step before acting is one way to create some distance and decrease impulsive behavior.

Reflect on Impulsivity

Use this exercise to reflect on impulsivity as it has affected you and consider times when impulsivity may be more or less beneficial, so you can manage it when necessary.

Think about a time when you acted impulsively. What were the positive and negative consequences of your actions?

_____

_____

_____

_____

_____

_____

Reflect on a time when you took more time to think before acting. What were the positive and negative consequences of your actions?

_____

_____

_____

_____

_____

_____

What are some situations in which it's helpful to act quickly and spontaneously?

_____

_____

_____

_____

_____

_____

_____

What are some situations in which it's better to think things through before acting?

_____

_____

_____

_____

_____

_____

_____

Go Slo-Mo

Try these simple but effective actions to slow down when you have an urge to react:

1. Say, "I need to think about it. Can I get back to you later?"

2. Paraphrase what the other person is saying. This buys you a little time as you repeat their words.

3. Journal about the situation before acting.

4. Take a short dopamine break by running, walking up a flight of stairs, or doing jumping jacks before you make a decision.

Experiencing strong emotions can be wonderful but sometimes overwhelming. I feel most comfortable when I am in control of my emotions and behavior. I can manage strong emotions and choose to act in ways that meet my goals. I mindfully choose my responses and behaviors.

Key Takeaways

This chapter presented a wide range of strategies to build your ADHD coping skills tool kit. We used some common struggles that women with ADHD have shared with us to build the strategies included in this chapter. This is not a complete list; you may face other struggles not covered here. However, please feel free to modify and adapt the skills and strategies listed here so they work for your unique needs. The main takeaway from this chapter is that however ADHD affects you, there are skills to help you manage your most bothersome symptoms.

Building an ADHD tool kit takes time and practice. The quick strategies outlined in this chapter are a great way to start tackling ADHD challenges in the areas of procrastination, time management, decision-making, motivation, emotion regulation, and impulse control. Here is a brief summary of the key skills introduced in each area and action steps so you can start strengthening these skills right away.

Procrastination

KEY SKILLS: Make to-do lists, divide large tasks into smaller pieces, use a body double, schedule catch-up time.

ACTION STEP: This week, try creating a daily and weekly to-do list. Which style is more helpful for you?

Time Management

KEY SKILLS: Create a realistic schedule, use a timer.

ACTION STEP: Today, estimate the amount of time a certain task will take. Then time yourself doing it. Do you tend to overestimate or underestimate? Knowing this will help you be more accurate when creating a schedule.

Disorganization

KEY SKILLS: Use checklists, practice decluttering, keep it simple.

ACTION STEP: This week, pick a section of your home or a personal object, like your bag, to organize. Make a checklist that you can reference whenever you need it.

Decision-Making

KEY SKILLS: Assess pros and cons, consider short- and long-term outcomes, avoid decision paralysis by making good-enough (rather than perfect) decisions.

ACTION STEP: Identify a decision you may be avoiding or delaying, and generate possible choices, pros, cons, and outcomes.

Motivation

KEY SKILLS: Set goals using the SMART format, create visual representations of these goals to inspire you.

ACTION STEP: Today, write out one SMART goal (specific, measurable, achievable, relevant, and time-bound) for yourself.

Emotion Regulation

KEY SKILLS: Calm your nervous system, give your logical brain time to catch up with your emotional brain.

ACTION STEP: This month, experiment with multiple strategies to calm your nervous system. Try deep breathing, meditation, progressive muscle relaxation, and patting cold water on your face. What works best to settle your body?

Impulse Control

KEY SKILLS: Pause, go slow.

ACTION STEP: This week, consciously pause or slow down in a situation in which you might normally act on impulse. How does this feel in the moment? In retrospect?

I can be independent and support myself in being the best version of me, but I also know how to ask for help when I need it. Asking for help and being willing to receive support from others is courageous and shows emotional maturity. Everyone can benefit from a combination of support from self and others. If I feel self-conscious about asking for help, I can remind myself: "Asking for help shows strength, not weakness. I will help myself by seeking support from others."

CHAPTER 5

Set Yourself Up for Success

In the last chapter, you practiced many helpful strategies to manage your ADHD. Now you'll learn how to cement your success by creating a system of support. Building a support network of friends, family, and people in your workplace with whom you can be mutually honest and authentic is helpful for everyone.

Many people, both with and without ADHD, struggle to ask others for help. In some cases, people say that asking for help feels like a weakness. Some women worry about bothering others, are shy, or are not sure how to ask for help. Pride and willfulness can also get in the way of asking for help, even when we need it. Shame and fear are two of the most powerful barriers to asking for help. And some women may be concerned that other people will not understand what they are going through. Every human being can benefit from help at one time or another. Having the wisdom to know when you need help and the courage to ask for it is truly a strength, not a weakness.

In this chapter, you'll be invited to think about different groups of people in your life who may be able to support your success. You'll then brainstorm and practice what you might want to disclose about your ADHD and to whom.

TALIA'S STORY

Talia, a 33-year-old software developer with ADHD, finds that she does her best work when she is able to spread it out over the course of a 12-hour day, taking breaks to exercise, eat, and spend time with family, rather than grinding straight through a typical eight-hour workday. Talia explained her work style to her boss. Talia asked if she would be able to leave work around 3:00 p.m. to exercise and have dinner and then finish the last few hours of her day from home, after 6:00 p.m. Her boss was initially reluctant, but agreed to a trial period. She was so impressed with the quality of work that Talia was able to maintain with this modified schedule that she allowed Talia to continue. Talia's boss also established flexible workplace hours for other employees, finding it improved the productivity of her team.

Getting Comfortable Asking for Help

In the last chapter, you learned techniques to manage ADHD and create your own ADHD tool kit. Practicing these skills by yourself can improve your life, but what can you do when your personal ADHD tool kit is not enough, and you need something more?

In these instances, it can be beneficial to ask for help and talk about how your brain works with friends, family, mental health clinicians, and, in some instances, coworkers or bosses. For some disenfranchised groups, like gender nonconforming or BIPOC women, asking for help can be more complicated, because they have a history of being misunderstood and mistreated in interpersonal relationships and by the medical community. For individuals from marginalized groups, it's vital to find safe people with similar identities or understanding allies who can help. Together, you can brainstorm solutions that will help you thrive. Consider one of our patients, Tenisha, who was able to find the strength to ask for help.

Tenisha is a 38-year-old tenure-track university professor. She has her own tool kit of strategies for managing ADHD. Tenisha worries about her career, and she works hard to prevent ADHD from getting in her way. She realizes that obtaining tenure is a long, arduous process, and her workplace has historically not been supportive of professors with learning differences. Each day, she makes a to-do list, breaks daily tasks into smaller chunks, and updates her checklist with completed deadlines and new deadlines for the many academic publications she juggles. These strategies have served Tenisha well at work, but they take a lot of emotional and mental energy. By the end of the day, Tenisha just wants to rest.

In her personal life, Tenisha doesn't worry as much about managing her ADHD. She has always had a close-knit group of friends. Friends tell her that she injects energy into any social situation and that they appreciate her spontaneity. However, some of her friendships were strained when Tenisha came late to planned events or missed important dates and details. Because her friends didn't know about Tenisha's ADHD, they took her lateness personally and felt hurt.

Although Tenisha cared about her friends deeply, her ADHD symptoms were interfering with her ability to remember details and times. Tenisha had not spent as much energy cultivating her ADHD tool kit in her social life. When she shared her diagnosis with her friends and explained that her ADHD makes her struggle with attention to detail and perceptions of time, it helped them see her behaviors in a different way.

Tenisha also worked to develop stronger listening and time-management skills to strengthen her friendships. It was difficult for Tenisha to share her diagnosis, but she discovered that it was a turning point in nourishing her relationships.

In Tenisha's case, she had good reasons to be hesitant about disclosing her ADHD diagnosis at work. Later in this chapter, we'll explore how to gauge if and how you can talk about ADHD with your colleagues and bosses. At the same time, Tenisha found strength and healing in disclosing her ADHD diagnosis to her friends.

Many women find that having conversations with their partners and other adult family members about how ADHD affects them is crucial for protecting the relationships and for deepening mutual understanding. A partner who understands how ADHD affects the relationship's communication, organization, and other aspects of life can empathize. As a result, they are likely to react with more compassion and provide more support when needed.

Moms with ADHD may see benefits in sharing their diagnosis with their children. ADHD tends to run in families, so sharing your experience and how you have overcome difficulties can resonate with your children and perhaps validate their own feelings and experiences.

For many friends and family members, learning more about what ADHD is and how it affects you can serve to build a lasting foundation of understanding and support.

Create a Disclosure Plan

Can you think of a situation in which disclosing your ADHD to someone could be helpful?

....

....

What are three positive changes that could come from sharing your ADHD in this situation?

1. ....

2. ....

3. ....

What are three internal barriers (feelings or concerns) that prevent you from seeking support from others?

1. ....

2. ....

3. ....

How can you reframe your perspective on these barriers? Try doing so here.

1. ....

2. ....

3. ....

What you do with this plan is entirely up to you. The exercise is designed to help you reflect on a potentially worthwhile place to share your diagnosis for increased understanding and support. You may choose to act on this, reflect on other potential areas for disclosure, or think on it a bit longer first. It's all movement in the right direction.

When Going It Alone Doesn't Cut It

There are times when using your ADHD skills and strategies will be enough to manage your ADHD. In other cases, ADHD symptoms may become so overwhelming that managing is difficult to do alone. Building your support network may involve making the decision to share your ADHD symptoms and/or diagnosis with friends, family members, and people in your workplace.

Throughout this section, think about the support you would like to receive from various people. In some instances, it may be easier to share specific symptoms, such as saying, "I struggle with focus" or "I have difficulty with organization." In other cases, you may choose to share your formal diagnosis of ADHD. You'll think about what you might choose to disclose to your parents, your children, other family members, and your friends, colleagues, and bosses. Who you choose to lean on for support is unique to you. What's right for one person may not be right for the next, and that's okay. Whatever your circumstances, use this chapter to work toward feeling empowered to talk with friends, family, colleagues, and bosses about how they can help you do your best.

DAHLIA'S STORY

Dahlia was diagnosed with ADHD at age 40, when she finally talked to a doctor about the trouble she was having staying focused and completing tasks in her job managing an art gallery. She used her wonderful sense of color, composition, and style to curate a gallery full of beautiful works of art that gallery patrons loved. However, during lengthy meetings with her business partner about running the business side of the gallery, such as financials, policies, and procedures, she found herself zoning out and thinking of other things. She felt embarrassed if she had to ask her colleague to repeat something because she was distracted during their conversation. She eventually saw a psychiatrist and was treated for ADHD, which significantly reduced her symptoms.

Dahlia wished she had been able to get help earlier for her ADHD, because she now recognized how much distractibility and poor focus had negatively affected her when she was a young girl in school. She was apprehensive about sharing her experience with her teenage children, but when she did, she was able to validate her 13-year-old daughter's experience of ADHD and set the example that it is okay to ask for help. It felt good for both of them to have open communication about ADHD, and now her daughter is getting the support she needs as well.

Talking to Friends

Sharing your ADHD experience with friends is a personal choice. Sometimes sharing information about how ADHD impacts you can improve understanding and deepen the relationship. An explanation of how ADHD affects you can shift how your friends look at issues that may come up between you. You may also end up finding out that some of your friends also have ADHD or struggle with learning differences or mental health challenges. When you open up, you may also inspire them to seek support for their own struggles. There is strength in vulnerability in relationships, because it allows for deeper connection and closeness—after all, we are all human. Check out the Resources (page 121) for some books that teach more about vulnerability.

Gail, a postal worker, uses humor to talk about ADHD in her social circle. For example, when Gail mixed up times for a get-together, she laughed, "I guess I haven't totally conquered my ADHD yet!" Gail found it was important to establish patience around communication with friends. She did so by explaining that it may take her longer to respond to messages than neurotypical people, or she may completely miss a text message or email. She gives new friends a heads-up that she's not on social media, and if she misses a text or email, to please just message her again.

There are countless approaches you can take to share your story. Like Gail, some people use levity and humor. Others are more serious when they talk about their mental health. No matter how you choose to talk about your ADHD, be kind to yourself and make sure it feels comfortable and authentic to you.

When you're preparing to open up to friends, it can be helpful to think through what kind of support you are looking for. For example, if you are looking for help with problem-solving, it might be best to choose a friend who is analytical and solution-oriented to talk with. If you need a friend to vent to about your frustrations with ADHD, an empathetic friend would be a great choice. If you want to try body-doubling with a friend (page 55), figure out who is working on similar tasks as you, and who might be willing to set up time together as an accountability partner.

Depending on what you choose to disclose to friends, consider your privacy preferences. For example, if you prefer to keep your diagnosis private, you might say, "Please don't share this with anyone." Conversely, if you are very comfortable talking about your ADHD, you could say, "I am open about my ADHD, so there is no need to keep this private." This way, friends will understand your sentiments regarding how to handle the personal health information you've shared.

Asking for Help from Friends

Use this exercise to practice thinking about what kind of support you'd like from friends, who you would want to talk to, and what you might say.

What kind of support would you like from friends around your ADHD?

....

....

Name three people you might turn to for this help and why.

1. ....

2. ....

3. ....

Brainstorm three scripts detailing how you'd start the conversation about your ADHD.

1. ....

....

....

2. ....

....

....

3. ....

....

....

Talking to Colleagues (Especially Your Boss)

When faced with the idea of talking about ADHD symptoms or diagnosis at work, many women express conflicted feelings and fears about the risk of discrimination at work. We'll talk about both options of sharing and not sharing your diagnosis so you can make an informed decision on this front.

SHARE YOUR SYMPTOMS BUT NOT YOUR CLINICAL DIAGNOSIS

When you share your ADHD symptoms that might impact you with your coworkers or boss without sharing your diagnosis, you may focus on things like distractedness, restlessness, or hyperfocus. It can help to frame these in a positive light. For example, if you are physically hyperactive and need movement breaks, you could say something like "I've noticed my best ideas come to me during walks. I'd like to take a short walk several times a day to keep my mind fresh." If you struggle with distractedness, you might say, "I work best in a quiet space with minimal disruptions." If you tend to hyperfocus, you could say, "I'm able to bring laser focus to some types of tasks."

Harper, a 28-year-old assistant editor, often needed to collaborate with her colleagues in the publishing industry. She shared with her coworker, "I tend to be sensitive to noise distractions when working. I like to wear these noise-canceling headphones, so I may not hear you if you say my name softly. Please feel free to tap me on the shoulder anytime—I'm always happy to collaborate!" She also asked her boss, "I work best early in the morning and when I have an uninterrupted chunk of time that allows me to focus. Would it be okay for me to not answer emails and calls between 8:00 and 11:00 a.m. so I can use that time for reading and editing manuscripts?" This helped her set expectations about her most effective work habits and collaboratively problem-solve if they had a different expectation or need.

SHARE YOUR ADHD DIAGNOSIS DIRECTLY

Choosing to share any diagnosis at work comes with potential risks and benefits. On one hand, if your boss and/or colleague understands the ways your ADHD may give you a leg up and how it can get in your way, it allows them to provide support that suits you. Some articles by ADHD specialists suggest that if you are anticipating facing performance problems at work due to your ADHD, it may be best to disclose the diagnosis up front, before performance problems are flagged by your employer.

On the other hand, you may face discrimination in the workplace if you disclose medical issues of any kind, including ADHD. The Americans with Disabilities Act (ADA) protects against workplace discrimination, but does not apply in all scenarios, such as at very small companies, or if your ADHD does not meet the threshold to be considered a disability. ADA.gov, ADDitudemag.com, and CHADD.org have additional information about ADHD as a disability and anti-discrimination law. See page 121 for specific links to these resources.

DO YOU NEED TO INVOLVE HR?

The Americans with Disabilities Act (ADA) is a law passed by the US government in 1990 that protects individuals with disabilities from workplace discrimination. Not all people with ADHD qualify as disabled, but ADHD that causes limiting functional impairments is considered a disability under the ADA. This means if ADHD impairs one or more major life functions and yet you retain the ability to perform essential job functions, your workplace may be required to enact reasonable accommodations for you at work. Your workplace would be required to provide accommodations under this law only if your diagnosis and disability have been formally disclosed. This is one reason why some people choose to reveal their ADHD to their company's human resources (HR) department.

Some people fear that involving HR and asking for accommodations because of ADHD could have negative consequences or cause discrimination at work. Although we wish it weren't the case, we know this can sometimes occur. Because there are numerous caveats and nuances to the ADA, it may be useful to consult an employment lawyer about your specific situation before talking with HR.

If you do speak to HR, first think about what accommodations would help you most. For some women, having a quiet or separate work space is helpful. Others may benefit from the ability to take frequent, brief breaks. Women with ADHD come up with creative solutions to optimize their efficiency in the workplace, and a supportive work environment can facilitate increased productivity and morale.

Map a Support at Work Plan

Use this exercise to brainstorm reasonable changes in your workplace that would help you thrive. Then think about concrete ways to move forward with these changes.

List up to three things you would change in your workplace to help you do your best work.

1. ....

2. ....

3. ....

Who would you need to talk to make these changes?

....

....

....

Are these things that you could ask for without disclosing your ADHD? If so, how would you ask?

....

....

....

If you feel you would need to disclose your ADHD diagnosis, who would you talk to first? What would you say?

....

....

....

Talking to Adult Family Members

You may choose to share your diagnosis with your entire family, no one at all, or select individuals. Sharing your diagnosis with your spouse may be particularly helpful, if not necessary, as spouses tend to interact closely around some of the things that ADHD can impact most. Some of our patients have shared that trouble with organization, time management, and attention to detail dramatically impact their home life and relationship with their partner. Some women reported that their partners became frustrated with them or couldn't understand the troubles they were having until they better understood ADHD. By understanding that ADHD is a brain condition that can cause changes in brain chemicals and neural pathways that control attention, focus, impulse control, planning, and reward behaviors, your partner and other family members can better relate to you and your needs.

Sharing your ADHD diagnosis with siblings may benefit them, because they are more likely to have ADHD as a first-degree relative. If they can relate to your ADHD on a personal level, they may consider getting tested and treated themselves. Regardless, the support of your siblings and other family members can be pivotal in tackling the challenges of ADHD.

Once you share your diagnosis, family members may have questions. If your family members want to learn more information than you can provide, look to the Resources (page 121) for links to the Centers for Disease Control and Prevention (CDC) and the National Institute of Mental Health (NIMH).

If you are choosing to share your ADHD diagnosis with your parents, grandparents, or other older relatives, it's important to be aware of potential generational divides around views of mental health diagnoses and treatment in general. Mental health diagnoses tended to be more stigmatized in the past, and previous generations tended to be far less open about mental health troubles. Generation Z individuals (born between 1997 and 2012) have experienced a less stigmatized view of learning differences and mental health disorders than earlier generations. Generation Z is more likely to acknowledge and seek help for mental health concerns in this context. If your parent or family member does not seem initially open to learning about your ADHD, you can try gently sharing general information with them about ADHD and how it specifically affects you. You might also choose not to pursue further conversations about ADHD with that person if you feel it won't help them support you or improve your relationship. Remember, you get to make the decision about how much and with whom you share.

TALKING TO CHILDREN
ABOUT YOUR ADHD

Because ADHD can run in families, talking with your kids about the symptoms you've experienced as a child and/or as an adult may validate some of their own similar experiences. Even if they don't struggle with similar symptoms, disclosing your diagnosis to kids in an age-appropriate way can help them understand you better. By sharing your challenges with your children and talking about what you have done to cope, you open the door for future conversations on the subject. This can also help with any challenges with neurodiversity that may arise for them or around them in the future. By being honest with them, you have the chance to teach and inspire them to talk about struggles without shame or fear.

When talking to a young child, you might say something like "Mommy uses lists to help her keep track of details that can be tricky to remember." For a slightly older child, you could say something like "My brain moves really fast; sometimes I say things without thinking. I'm working on slowing down and thinking things through." By middle school, many kids could understand a more direct disclosure such as "I have ADHD. This means I sometimes get distracted or have trouble focusing." You can also reassure them that ADHD is common and just means that your brain works a little differently. This would also be a great time to share some of the benefits of your particular neurodiversity with your children, as you explain some of the strengths that come with your diagnosis.

Open the Door to Discussion

Think about what you might choose to share with your children about your ADHD. Try to include at least one benefit of your neurodiversity. If you have children of different ages, you can brainstorm different scripts to match their developmental level. Brainstorm what you might say here:

_____

_____

_____

_____

_____

If you have trouble getting started, here are a few prompts:

"I want to talk with you about the way my brain works."

"My brain ["moves really fast," "jumps around quickly," etc.]."

"For me this means [a positive trait of your ADHD] and sometimes [a challenge of your ADHD]."

"You might have noticed that I _____. This is part of my ADHD."

"If I am having trouble because of my ADHD, I [positive coping skill]."

You can explain that everyone's brain works a little differently, and that is okay, and that ADHD does not limit you—you can do anything you want to do in life with ADHD. Finish by opening the door for any questions. When you are done creating your script, read it over and make any changes that feel more authentic to your situation.

PARENTING WITH ADHD

Parenting is the challenge of a lifetime, and having ADHD can add additional complexity. Some parents with ADHD say that trouble with organization and time management can lead them to lose track of kids' schedules or miss deadlines. Others say trouble with inattention means they can sometimes zone out or feel distracted at home and with family. Helpful strategies include keeping to-do lists (page 55), making realistic schedules (page 58), and using checklists (page 60). Parenting can also be a wonderful place to get support from people in your life. If you have a co-parent, consider talking through each partner's strengths and weaknesses and try to share parenting tasks accordingly. Asking friends and family members to support you in parenting with ADHD can also be a wonderful use of your support network.

In general, my friends, family, and coworkers want to support me. They help me in being the best version of myself. It can feel scary to ask for support, but I can remind myself that people care about me and want to help. If I feel reluctant to go to my support network for help, I can remind myself, "People care about me and want to help me do my best."

Key Takeaways

This chapter discussed how and when to ask for help and empower you to ask for help. You considered the people from whom you might seek help with the challenges of ADHD, including friends, family, and people in your workplace. We talked about several approaches to asking for help, including sharing your ADHD diagnosis or just describing the symptoms you are having. We touched on the fears some women have expressed about sharing their ADHD diagnosis, and you were invited to reflect on your own fears and internal barriers to seeking support. Beyond getting help and support from others, sharing about your ADHD with others helps them understand you better and destigmatize ADHD and neurodivergence in general. Ultimately, sharing health information is a personal choice, and each woman has the right to decide whether, how, when, and with whom to share. How would you like to build your support system? Consider the following action steps that can help you get started.

- Brainstorm a list of help or support you'd like from others around your ADHD. Be as specific as possible.

....

....

- List the family members from whom you might want to seek support around your ADHD. What kind of support would you like from them?

....

....

- List the friends with whom you might consider sharing about your ADHD. What might you choose to share with each?

....

....

- List those people in your workplace with whom you would consider sharing your ADHD diagnosis or symptoms. What are the pros and cons of sharing with each?

....

....

....

Professional help is available to me. I can speak to a mental health clinician who will understand my concerns and know how to help. Experts are used to speaking with women with similar concerns. I feel great about getting help for ADHD and knowing that much research has been conducted on ADHD to guide my treatment.

CHAPTER 6

Seeking Professional Support and Making Lifestyle Changes

In the last few chapters, you developed a tool kit of ADHD coping skills and practiced getting comfortable with seeking support from your community of friends, family, and coworkers.

Skills and social support are essential for managing ADHD. However, there are times when additional treatment is beneficial to address moderate to severe ADHD symptoms that impact your functioning in various areas of your life. Seeking professional treatment when needed shows strength and resolve, and different forms of therapy and medications have helped many women with ADHD adapt to stressors and improve their well-being. Historically marginalized groups, such as BIPOC and LGBTQIA+ identified women, have faced stigmatization by the medical establishment, and members of such groups may feel skeptical about seeking professional help. These concerns are understandable. It may be worthwhile to seek medical care from professionals who identify similarly or have a strong track record as allies.

This chapter outlines professional treatment options available for women with ADHD and is just an introduction to all the resources out there. If or when you choose treatment, talk with a mental health clinician who understands ADHD and can make personalized recommendations for addressing treating your symptoms. In addition to professional support, lifestyle changes including stress reduction, scheduling, healthy nutrition, exercise, and sleep can also help minimize ADHD symptoms and optimize your ability to thrive in all areas of life.

DEVON'S STORY

Devon, a 26-year-old medical student, was diagnosed with ADHD in college. She used organizational and time-management skills she learned online to stay on track. She also asked for support from her study groups and professors, which helped. However, when Devon began medical school, she found the demands even greater than in college. The coping strategies she had used in college were still helpful, but Devon felt that her ADHD was increasingly affecting her academic functioning. She decided to seek professional support for her ADHD. Devon's therapist used neurofeedback (see page 100) and provided executive function coaching. Eventually, she saw a psychiatric nurse practitioner who prescribed medication. Instead of working overtime to manage ADHD symptoms alone, Devon felt relieved to have support and professional help, in addition to her own coping skills, to help her do her best in school.

Professional Support

There are several effective clinical treatments for ADHD. What works for one person may not be the best choice for another. Your ADHD treatment plan should be unique, just like you! This plan should consider your symptoms, your preferences, and the treatments available.

Treatment can include lifestyle changes, therapy, and medications. Therapy for ADHD usually includes building skills and strategies to manage the symptoms that impact you most. A therapist can coach you in organization and planning and developing skills to support focus, relationships, and emotion regulation.

Medications are an important treatment option for ADHD treatment. The two main categories of medication for ADHD are stimulants and non-stimulants. Stimulant medications, typically recommended as the first-line treatment for ADHD, are highly effective and generally well tolerated. When researchers look at the effect of medication on ADHD symptoms, they see a substantial reduction in ADHD symptoms in about 70 percent of adults who take the medications. Most people tolerate ADHD medication well, although mild side effects such as appetite suppression are common, and major side effects can occur. Reflect on your preferences and speak to your clinician about your treatment options.

ADHD often goes hand in hand with other mental health concerns. Research shows that over 30 percent of adults with ADHD have another diagnosis such as depression, anxiety, substance abuse, or other mental health conditions. It is the job of mental health clinicians to help with whatever concerns you bring to the table. Your clinician will be better able to help you if you share whatever issues you are experiencing.

When to Seek Therapy

Therapy is a pivotal treatment for women with ADHD who find that their own coping skills and support systems are not enough to effectively manage their ADHD symptoms. Trained mental health clinicians, including psychiatrists, psychiatric nurse practitioners, psychologists, mental health counselors, and social workers, can help women with ADHD by providing a variety of proven interventions for ADHD. Therapy options include neurofeedback, cognitive training, psychotherapy, and coaching.

Neurofeedback is a type of therapy that trains your brain to operate in beta wave frequency. Beta waves are a type of electrical brain activity associated with concentration. People with ADHD tend to have fewer beta waves in key areas of the brain than neurotypical people. They also have an excess of slower theta waves, which are associated with daydreaming, creativity, and intuition. Neurofeedback uses technology to show you on a screen a visual representation of the predominant brain wave frequencies in key areas of the brain. Using exercises and games, you learn how to shift your brain waves to beta frequency, which allow for focus and concentration. A review of research on neurofeedback and ADHD published in 2020 concluded that neurofeedback is an effective treatment for ADHD, about as effective as antidepressants for depression.

Cognitive training involves being coached in and practicing executive functioning skills such as planning, impulse control, memory, and organization. Research indicates that cognitive training is most effective in improving a person's working memory.

If you are among the 30 percent of women with ADHD who struggle with a second mental health condition, such as anxiety or depression, therapy may be especially useful for you. Research evidence shows that therapy can help significantly reduce anxious and depressive symptoms.

Once you've made the decision to seek out therapy, the next step is to find a therapist who is a good fit. This can take some effort. Websites such as PsychologyToday .com and GoodTherapy.org can help you sift through potential clinicians to find a good match and to find clinicians who self-identify as specializing in ADHD. Filtering by location, insurances accepted, out-of-pocket costs, and treatment approach can be especially useful. Your primary care clinician can also be a great resource, as they often have a network of trusted mental health professionals they refer to. If you have insurance, you can call your insurance company for a list of in-network mental health clinicians, although this will not necessarily give you information about whether they specialize in the treatment of ADHD—a phone call or website visit can provide more information. You can also ask friends and family members for recommendations.

If you are uninsured, accessibility of care will vary depending on where you live. Your best bet is to look into federally qualified health centers in your area, as well as contacting your local or county human services department to inquire about free or sliding-scale mental health services in your area. For additional options, see the Resources (page 121) for a link to a directory of free and low-cost counseling resources.

Finding a clinician who is available, takes your insurance or meets your financial requirements, and is a good fit can take time and effort. Please give it your best effort—there are many wonderful mental health clinicians out there, and the benefits of finding the right support are worth every bit of effort.

WHAT IF WE'RE NOT A FIT?

I f you feel your clinician is not a good fit, it is often helpful to bring up your concerns in a session to see if they can be addressed. Sometimes trouble that arises inside the therapy room can also reflect what is happening in your outside life. Being able to talk through concerns with your clinician can be a healing experience. If you don't want to continue with your clinician, you can always seek a second opinion or perspective by reaching out to another clinician. When possible, it may be helpful to do a brief consult with a few clinicians before deciding who you'll work with.

When to Seek Medication

If ADHD is interfering with your functioning at home, at work, or in relationships, consider having a conversation with a medical professional about the possibility of treating your ADHD with medication. The decision is yours and yours alone to make, and gathering all the knowledge you can will help you make the most informed decision. Discuss your medication options and the risks and benefits of each medication with your clinician. Feel free to ask any questions you may have. Several different types of medication are shown to effectively treat ADHD. This section will provide some basic information about medication options for ADHD.

STIMULANT MEDICATIONS

Stimulant medications are the most effective treatment for ADHD. Stimulants can improve focus and decrease distractibility and hyperactivity. They work by regulating norepinephrine and dopamine in the brain (see page 10), and work within about 30 minutes. There are two main types of stimulants—methylphenidates and amphetamines—with several medications in each of these two groups. Like all medications, stimulants can have side effects. The most common side effects are a lack of appetite, stomach discomfort, headaches, difficulty falling asleep, and irritability when the medication wears off.

Both short-acting and long-acting stimulant medications are available. The shorter-acting medications may last four hours, and some of the long-acting ones can work for up to 12 hours. How long the medicine works after you take it depends on the medicine and how your body processes it. Some women process medication very quickly, and others process it more slowly. Figuring out what works best for you will probably take some time. If you are trying a new medication, communicate with your prescriber about how you are feeling and managing on that specific medication and dosage.

NON-STIMULANT MEDICATIONS

Although stimulant medications are the most effective medications for ADHD, some people cannot tolerate them or prefer not to take them. Here, your prescriber may recommend a non-stimulant medication, which is also effective for ADHD symptoms. Common non-stimulant medications include atomoxetine, clonidine, and guanfacine.

Atomoxetine works by increasing norepinephrine and may also increase dopamine. This medicine can start to work right away to some degree, but can take up to three months to reach its full effect. The most common potential side effects of atomoxetine are dry mouth, headache, and gastrointestinal symptoms; however, most people don't have any side effects with this medication and it is generally well tolerated.

Clonidine and guanfacine can reduce hyperactivity, irritability, and impulsivity, and they improve focus, but to a lesser degree than stimulant medications. The medications have some immediate effects and some delayed effects. They block part of the stress response and therefore can reduce stress. Common potential side effects include dry mouth, fatigue, dizziness, and headaches.

As you can see, many treatment options exist for addressing ADHD symptoms—the key is to determine which formula works best for you. Sometimes a single treatment such as therapy is sufficient, and for some people, a combination of therapy, medications, and lifestyle changes will deliver the best results.

Is It Time for Professional Help?

Making the choice to seek professional help for ADHD depends on how much your symptoms are impacting your functioning. Use the following exercise to determine how much your symptoms currently impact you at home, school, work, and interpersonally.

At home, my ADHD impacts my ability to _____.

On a scale of 1 to 10 (10 being the most severe), how much does this bother you? _____

At school and/or work, my ADHD impacts my ability to _____.

On a scale of 1 to 10, how much does this bother you? _____

In my relationships, my ADHD impacts my ability to _____.

On a scale of 1 to 10, how much does this bother you? _____

I think I may have a second mental health condition besides ADHD. YES / NO

If so, specify suspected condition or other symptoms. _____

Reflect on what you've recorded here. Do you think it makes sense for you to seek professional help based on your answers? YES / NO

Key Takeaways

Though it may feel like a big decision, seeking professional support for ADHD or conditions that commonly co-occur with ADHD, such as anxiety or depression, can be a pivotal step in helping you achieve optimal health. It may take time and effort to develop a treatment plan that is right for you, but in the long run having done so will save you time, money, stress, and other health complications. You are worth the effort!

First, assess if you think you could benefit from professional help for your ADHD or additional mental health symptoms by completing the exercise on page 29. If you've answered yes or are not sure, consider these two additional action steps:

- For therapy, reach out to a trained and licensed therapist, such as a mental health counselor, social worker, or psychologist. Note that some psychiatrists and psychiatric nurse practitioners also offer therapy for ADHD. Some therapists offer a free five-minute phone consultation to see if you and the therapist are a good fit.

- For medication, reach out to a qualified medical professional, such as a psychiatrist or psychiatric nurse practitioner.

Lifestyle Changes to Improve ADHD

Lifestyle changes are a key part of addressing ADHD. Research documents the positive impact of healthy diet, good sleep habits, and stress-reduction practices on ADHD symptoms. Developing a lifestyle that works for your unique mind, body, and environment is a long-term project, and as you and your life circumstances change, you may need to make adjustments to your daily life habits. It's common knowledge that sleeping enough, eating a healthy diet, and exercising are good for health; however, figuring out how exactly to make those habits stick in the long run is challenging for many.

Because ADHD often comes with organizational difficulties, it may take extra effort to sort out your lifestyle habits. Making small and sustainable adjustments in your sleep, food, exercise, and other health habits adds up over time. Even if you make a 5 percent improvement in a year, after a few years that will add up. In general, it is better to make changes that fit you and your life and are sustainable for many years than to engage briefly in unsustainable programs. This might look like making a small modification, such as eating more vegetables, rather than going on a three-day juice cleanse. You will benefit from better lifestyle habits within days, and the benefits will add up over time. Most people notice feeling better on day one of a simple regimen of getting a good night of sleep, eating clean and healthy, and engaging in moderate exercise or movement.

Research shows that lifestyle changes make a tremendous difference for long-term health. Individuals who prioritize daily health habits such as refraining from smoking and excessive alcohol intake, eating well, sleeping enough, and exercising live longer and enjoy better health with fewer years of disability and illness. Remind yourself of your long-term life goals and build up your motivation for taking good care of yourself now and over the years. Slow and steady adds up to progress, and often the most lasting kind.

CORA'S STORY

Cora, a 36-year-old hairdresser with ADHD, realized that she needed to take better care of herself when the stress of her work and personal life began causing physical tension and headaches. She cared for her ill father, worked hard to maintain a full book of clients, and valued time spent with her wife and son. Cora's ADHD made managing time more difficult, and she found her stress level continually rising.

To counter her stress, Cora began working on improving her time-management skills. She also started to practice yoga every day for 30 minutes at home using a phone app. She found that this was brief enough to fit into her days. In addition, Cora started enjoying a cup of tea and a handful of nuts in the mornings, rather than skipping breakfast, and ordering a salad with protein and olive oil for lunch, rather than fast food. She quickly noticed her energy levels and mood were better on the days she nourished her body. Yoga and a healthier diet helped her feel more resilient and better able to enjoy her work and personal life.

Stress Management

Research indicates that people with ADHD experience a greater quantity of stressful life events and higher subjective perceptions of stress. But it's important to point out that stress is not always bad. Stress can alert us to pay attention to and prepare for something important, such as a big exam or meeting with the boss. The human body is resilient, and we have built-in mechanisms for dealing with stress. However, we also know that too much stress can have negative effects on our body and brain.

A healthy lifestyle improves resiliency in the face of stress. In addition, a tool kit of stress-management techniques that fit your temperament and preferences will help you cope and adapt when there are a lot of demands on you. There are hundreds of good stress-management techniques, such as mindfulness and mindful movement, various self-soothing strategies that balance stressful events with positive experiences, and anything else that allows you to get into a relaxed, calm, and centered space—a quick online search will bring up a wealth of information and resources on the subject. These strategies won't eliminate stress altogether, but they will help you manage stress in a healthy way and reduce the negative impact of stress on your life.

It is important, over time, to build your life in a way that fits you and make life choices that will protect you from excess stress. By managing your stress, you'll be better able to maintain focus, avoid impulsivity, and minimize irritability. It is also easier to tap into your hyperfocus skills when you are good at managing stress. Productivity and performance increase with mild stress but plummet with high stress levels.

MINDFULNESS

Mindfulness is a general term that encompasses many different practices, all with the goal of cultivating awareness of the present moment. Mindfulness practices may include meditation, yoga, breathing exercises, and mindful movement, to name a few. Research has shown that mindfulness practices can reduce stress, improve focus, reduce anxiety and depression symptoms, improve empathy, and even make your brain grow (cortical thickness and density of cells in certain areas of the brain is improved by mindfulness practice). These benefits emerge even with relatively short periods of intentionally mindful behavior.

One way to start exploring mindfulness practices is to take slow deep breaths through your nose, combined with extended exhales through your mouth or nose.

When practicing this, aim to make your exhale twice as long as your inhale or pretend to breathe out of a straw to slow your exhale. This breathing practice is one of many that can calm your central nervous system.

There are many in-person and online mindfulness and stress management courses available throughout the United States and around the world. There are also many apps that can help you to develop and cultivate a mindfulness practice. See Resources (page 121) for recommendations.

SELF-SOOTHING

Self-soothing is another key strategy for managing stress. Self-soothing can look different for different individuals—some women say that listening to music or watching a favorite movie is soothing, and others find hiking or being in nature more effective. Even among the three authors of this book, Kathleen uses lavender essential oil for self-soothing, Beata chooses to spend time in nature, and Christy finds putting her hands under running water an effective self-soothing strategy. The goal of self-soothing is to bring some comfort, in whatever healthy form works for you.

Identify three things you can do to soothe yourself. Make sure at least one of them is free and accessible in any situation.

1. ....

2. ....

3. ....

BALANCING

The third tip we'll introduce to manage stress is being conscious of balancing stressful events with positive or pleasant experiences. For example, if you are experiencing high levels of stress in your romantic relationship, balance it with time enjoyed with supportive friends, which can help you manage the relationship stress. Likewise, if you are feeling physically stressed and run-down, balancing your fatigue with a pleasant experience, such as massage or a warm bath, may be helpful.

Take a Relaxing Time-Out

We often hear "just breathe" as a response to stressful events—but that's because it works! This exercise involving controlled breathing offers a calming "time-out" from chaotic moments and may become a regular part of your relaxation practices.

1. Find a comfortable seated position in a chair. Sit up straight and place both feet flat on the floor.

2. Close your eyes, or gaze softly at a point a few feet in front of you.

3. Place one hand on your abdomen.

4. Take a deep inhale through your nose. With your hand, feel your abdomen fill like a balloon.

5. Exhale your breath slowly through your mouth. Extend your exhale about twice as long as your inhale, or pretend to exhale through a straw.

6. Repeat steps 4 and 5 for about two minutes. Gradually extend this period over time.

Overscheduling

Overscheduling is a common challenge for women with ADHD. If you struggle with impulsivity, maybe you say yes to too many activities and end up overscheduling yourself. The cultural pressure for women to say yes and accommodate others may also contribute to overscheduling. For those with attention and planning difficulties, you might not notice that you're overscheduled until it's too late! Following are some tips for freeing up your schedule.

BE KIND TO YOURSELF

Many women with ADHD are overscheduled and overwhelmed. In our society, girls and women are often raised with the expectation that they should do unpaid housework and caregiving on top of a typical paid job. This pressure can lead women to become self-critical and label themselves as "lazy" when they struggle to keep up with house and work. But that's so far from the truth! Don't fall into a self-blame trap. Instead of saying "I'm lazy" or "I have to do this," try "I'm in control" and "I'm choosing to do this."

You don't have to measure success by how many items you've checked off your checklist. Try measuring success by considering your values and what gives you pleasure, and strive to live in a way that will bring you closer to that big picture. When it comes to tasks that are not in alignment with your big picture, free yourself of excessive expectation and you'll be able to free up your schedule as well. Our patient Akemi realized that spending quality time biking with her child after dinner was more in alignment with her values than ensuring that all the dishes were washed, dried, and put away each night.

DON'T SWEAT IT; DELEGATE IT!

When you're feeling overscheduled, remember that you don't have to give in to societal pressure to "do it all." Lean into your existing networks at home and outside the home, and let your friends, family, and trusted peers know what they can do to help. Just as it can feel good when you extend help to others and have it accepted, allow your loved ones to extend that kindness to you. You deserve to be held and supported by people who care about you.

Take inventory of your strengths, weaknesses, and preferences, too. No one is good at everything! Maybe you're a fabulous dishwasher but a terrible cook. Offer to wash the dishes if someone else in the household does the cooking, or share responsibility for meals by picking up a healthy meal twice a week at the local grocery store.

WORK GENTLY, REWARD OFTEN

The hardest part of any job is getting started. Set yourself up for success by determining how you work best. First thing in the morning or after an afternoon nap? In a quiet room or a bustling café? One strategy is to plan on doing just five minutes of work. That makes it less overwhelming to get started. Once you are working, it's easier to keep going.

Also, remember that no task should go unrewarded! Design reward breaks into your schedule. Take a brief stroll in your neighborhood, make some afternoon tea, listen to a favorite song, or start that weekly yoga class you've been meaning to take. This will make you more efficient and allow you to spend more of your free time doing enjoyable things.

Divide and Conquer

In this exercise, you'll learn how to prioritize your schedule with a simple 2x2 table. This is also known as the Eisenhower Matrix, named after former US president Dwight D. Eisenhower, who said, "What is important is seldom urgent and what is urgent is seldom important."

Begin by making a weekly task list. If you're able to break a bigger, complex task into smaller, easier tasks, do it! Divide your list of weekly tasks into the four categories in the following table. Think of important tasks as things that contribute to your long-term goals and urgent tasks as things that need to be done immediately. Complete the tasks that are both important and urgent first. Schedule important and less urgent tasks over the course of the week. You can even delegate less important and urgent tasks to others. Finally, reduce less important and less urgent tasks.

	IMPORTANT	LESS IMPORTANT
URGENT	EXAMPLE: *Review serious lab abnormalities from this week with patients.*	EXAMPLE: *Call patients to remind of appointments.*
LESS URGENT	EXAMPLE: *Attend professional development conferences to maintain license.*	EXAMPLE: *Finish watching this season of Grey's Anatomy.*

Diet, Nutrition, and Exercise

Healthy diet and exercise are essential components of a healthy lifestyle, as well as of ADHD treatment. They will support all parts of you, including optimal brain function. Drinking lots of water will also help your body stay healthy. Some women have noticed that as they make incremental changes in their diet to reduce sugar and increase whole foods (foods in or close to their natural state), they notice a reduction in their ADHD symptoms. You don't have to make big changes overnight; small changes that you can sustain over time often work even better! Start by working to limit sugar and processed carbohydrates in your diet and increase your consumption of whole foods, healthy fats (such as nuts and seeds, avocado, and olive oil), and healthy protein (like eggs, beans, yogurt, seafood, and lean meat and poultry).

Some preliminary research suggests that people with ADHD may have lower blood levels of magnesium and iron. These deficiencies may not cause ADHD, but doctors may test your blood for nutrient levels and then suggest dietary supplements to improve general health and function.

It's no surprise that exercise and movement promote physical and mental well-being. Researchers have suggested that exercise may have mechanisms of action similar to those of ADHD medications; specifically, that exercise may help ADHD symptoms by increasing dopamine and norepinephrine thought to be involved in attention, planning, organization, and movement. Working toward regular cardiovascular exercise is a great lifestyle choice that may also improve your ADHD symptoms.

What Habits Work for You?

Different diet and exercise routines work for different people. Try this journaling exercise to see what works best for you and your ADHD.

Use a notebook or a note-taking app on your phone to answer the following prompts each day this week to see how you feel overall and how your ADHD symptoms are impacted by your diet and exercise routine. Try making gradual changes in your habits over time, and log how they impact you. Once you consider which choices help you feel and function at your best, you can make conscious lifestyle choices that will make you feel great!

EXERCISE:

Record your exercise, the duration, and the effort required.

I did _____ for _____ minutes.

On a scale of 1 to 10 (10 being the most intense), how strenuous was this exercise?

(1) (2) (3) (4) (5) (6) (7) (8) (9) (10)

I felt _____ before exercising, and _____ afterward.

FOOD/DRINK INTAKE:

Record what you ate and drank, and the estimated times.

_____

_____

_____

_____

_____

_____

CONTINUED >

EMOTIONS:

Rate your best and worst feelings today on a scale of 1 to 10 (10 being the most intense).

Worst:

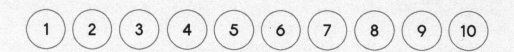

What time? ....

How did you feel? ....

How did you respond? ....

Best:

① ② ③ ④ ⑤ ⑥ ⑦ ⑧ ⑨ ⑩

What time? ....

How did you feel? ....

How did you respond? ....

SYMPTOMS:

Please rate your most severe ADHD symptoms today on a scale of 1 to 10 (10 being the most severe).

① ② ③ ④ ⑤ ⑥ ⑦ ⑧ ⑨ ⑩

Sleep Habits

A good night's rest helps your brain and body function well. Good sleep is important for women with and without ADHD. According to the CDC, adults between 18 and 60 years of age need a minimum of seven hours of sleep per night. You may find going to sleep difficult because it can be hard to settle your body and mind—this is common with ADHD. Following are some tips for promoting healthy sleep:

1. **CREATE A SLEEP SCHEDULE.** A consistent sleep schedule, in which you go to sleep each night and wake up each morning around the same time, is a key component of good sleep hygiene, particularly for those who struggle to fall or stay asleep.

2. **CREATE IDEAL SLEEP CONDITIONS.** Sleep quality can be improved by creating an environment that promotes restful sleep. Ideal sleep conditions include a cool, quiet, and dark space. To help provide the best environment for sleep, consider closing the blinds, using blackout curtains, and/or turning on a fan, white noise device, or white noise app on your phone.

3. **LIMIT CAFFEINE AND SCREEN TIME.** Certain substances and activities are known to interfere with good sleep, including caffeine and screen time. Many of us find it hard to disconnect from our devices, but research shows that looking at screens—phones, laptops, televisions, etc.—can negatively affect sleep. The blue light emitted from these screens is similar to the blue light emitted by the sun, and signals that it's time to be awake. Many sleep experts recommend eliminating screen use one hour before bed. If you enjoy coffee, tea, soda, or energy drinks, try to limit these to before midday, and switch to water, seltzer, decaffeinated coffee, or herbal tea in the afternoon.

Finally, if you struggle with falling or staying asleep, you may be feeling sleepy during the day. Although it may sound counterintuitive, a tip to improve sleep is to fight the urge to nap. Naps can feel wonderful, but they may reduce sleep drive in people struggling with insomnia. If you struggle with sleep, it's best to avoid naps.

Track and Improve Your Sleep

If you are not sure if you need to work on sleep, try tracking your sleep for one to two weeks to establish a baseline. Then try the following exercises and see if your sleep patterns change.

1. Set a bedtime and wake-up time that will work for you:

    Bedtime: ....

    Wake-up time: ....

2. Reduce daily caffeine intake.

3. Stop screens one hour before bed.

4. After one to two weeks, consider how your sleep has changed. Do you notice that it's easier to fall asleep? Stay asleep?

    ....

    ....

    ....

    ....

Key Takeaways

Hopefully, you walked away from this chapter with a good idea of how both professional support and lifestyle choices can help lessen ADHD symptoms.

We explored the types of therapy and medications that are available for women with ADHD. Therapy and medications may be particularly helpful for those who experience ADHD-related issues that cause significant trouble in one or more areas of their lives. Professional support can be especially helpful for women who have ADHD and a second mental health diagnosis, such as anxiety or depression. Medications may also be useful, but multiple factors go into the decision to start medicine. For example, a woman who is trying to conceive would consult with her psychiatrist regarding whether the potential risk to her baby would be balanced by the potential benefit of reducing her symptoms. Other health conditions as well as family history should also be considered when talking about medication. Be sure to discuss this as well as your own specific concerns and preferences.

In addition to therapy and medication options, you learned about how lifestyle choices can improve your well-being and focus. Taking good care of your body through a healthy diet and plenty of hydration, regular exercise, and adequate sleep feels good and supports mental and physical wellness. We discussed how stress management and reduced overscheduling can help lessen ADHD challenges. The following action steps are geared toward both considering professional help and making healthy lifestyle choices.

- Consider the idea of seeking professional help for your ADHD. Do you think you might benefit from therapy or medication management? If so, start to research local mental health clinicians (see page 121 for links to resources).

- Reduce sugar and increase healthy fats and protein in your diet this week. Notice how this makes you feel.

- Increase your exercise by 10 percent each week until you reach a goal of at least 20 minutes per day or 30 minutes five times per week.

- Eliminate screen time in the hour before bed. Does your sleep pattern change?

- Try at least one mindfulness or self-soothing practice today (page 106). How do you feel after doing this?

Lifestyle choices affect my health and well-being. The choices I make can positively impact my life and ADHD symptoms in a big way. I'm in control of my lifestyle choices, and I choose a lifestyle that supports my mental and physical health.

The Road Forward

Congratulations! You've reached the last section of *Managing ADHD Workbook for Women*.

Chapter 1 gave an overview of hyperactive, inattentive, and combined-type attention deficit hyperactivity disorder (ADHD) in women. You learned about how these conditions may show up in women and girls and why ADHD diagnoses may sometimes be missed in this population. ADHD affects women in different ways, including procrastination, loss of focus, and impulsive behavior. You also read about the potential impacts of ADHD on relationships, time management, decision-making, and emotion regulation. Such challenges are not a result of laziness or not caring, but rather symptoms of ADHD.

In chapter 2, you read more about the origins of ADHD, including that it commonly runs in families. You learned about the structural and chemical differences in the brain that are common to people with ADHD. You completed a self-evaluation of ADHD symptoms and learned about the specific criteria for diagnosing ADHD. We also addressed myths about ADHD, including the myth that people with ADHD are lazy or not intelligent. These are far from the truth. People with ADHD are as likely to be hardworking, intelligent, and accomplished as anyone else.

Chapter 3 focused on the beauty that neurodiversity, including ADHD, brings to our world. Understanding that neurodiversity such as ADHD can come with positives as well as challenges can allow you to lean into the strengths that come with your neurodiversity, including creativity, energy, and resilience. By feeling less pressure to approach things the same way that neurotypical people might, you can free yourself to achieve more.

Chapter 4 helped you develop a tool kit of ways to manage ADHD symptoms when they get in your way. If procrastination is an issue, you can add using lists, accountability partners, and chunking tasks to your tool kit. If time management is a concern, your tool kit now includes using timers and schedules to keep you on track. For women who have trouble making decisions, pro-and-con lists can help, as can efforts to make a good decision rather than a perfect decision. Setting SMART goals can help with motivation. Women who struggle with emotion regulation can stop, name their emotions, and calm their bodies. Finally, tools of pausing and going in slow motion can help with impulsive behaviors. With all these tools, the key is to practice them consciously at first so they eventually become a seamless and automatic part of your life.

In chapter 5, you were called on to consider asking for support. We explored women's reservations about sharing their ADHD and looked at ways of asking friends, family, and colleagues for help, with and without disclosing your specific diagnosis. You also learned about how the Americans with Disabilities Act may protect women with ADHD in the workplace. Many women fear that disclosing ADHD may result in discrimination at work; this is something to consider carefully and potentially discuss with an employment lawyer. However, most people in your family, friendships, and community are likely to be happy to understand you better and support you.

Finally, in chapter 6, we explored the idea of seeking professional help for ADHD and making lifestyle changes to promote health and wellness. You learned about therapy and medications that help reduce ADHD symptoms and lifestyle choices that optimize well-being. This chapter focused on getting help if needed and taking care of your body through good diet, sleep, exercise, and stress reduction.

Different elements of this book will resonate with different women. We encourage you to take what works for your unique set of symptoms and circumstances and leave the rest. You are a unique individual with power to use your ADHD to your advantage. You can use skills, lifestyle choices, and support from others in moments where ADHD challenges you. By completing this book, you invested in understanding your ADHD better so you can feel and function at your best. We are thrilled you chose to make this book a part of your journey and are excited to imagine what you'll do next, with all your knowledge and power!

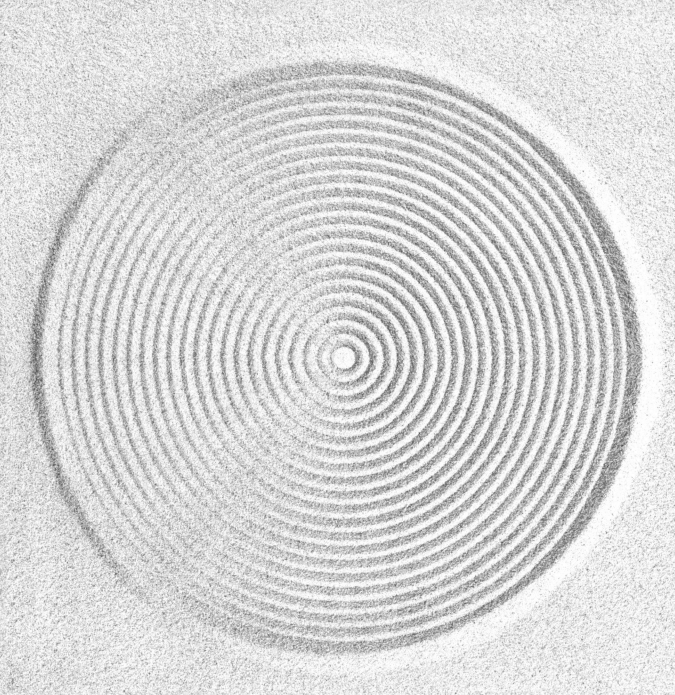

RESOURCES

The World Health Organization Adult ADHD Self-Report Scale

Find the eighteen-question ADHD Self-Report Scale online by searching for "The World Health Organization Adult ADHD Self-Report Scale" or "ASRS Screener." Here are three websites where you can find the assessment.

psychology-tools.com/adult-adhd-self-report-scale
apaservices.org/practice/reimbursement/health-registry/self-reporting-symp-ton-scale.pdf
add.org/wp-content/uploads/2015/03/adhd-questionnaire-ASRS111.pdf

Professional Organizations

American Academy of Child and Adolescent Psychiatry (AACAP) ADHD Resource Center
AACAP.org/aacap/Families_and_Youth/Resource_Centers/ADHD_Resource _Center/Home.aspx
This resource center on ADHD includes FAQs, clinical resources, age-appropriate books, and brief, informative articles called "Facts for Families."

American Psychiatric Association (APA)
Psychiatry.org/patients-families/adhd/what-is-adhd
The APA topic page on ADHD includes information about symptoms, diagnosis, and treatment, plus an expert Q&A and patient stories.

American Psychological Association (APA)
APA.org/topics/adhd
The APA's topic page on ADHD includes informative articles and podcast episodes, as well as APA-published books about ADHD.

Nonprofit Organizations

Attention Deficit Disorder Association (ADDA)
ADD.org
ADDA is an inclusive community that supports ADHD adults. In addition to education and advocacy, the ADDA hosts virtual support groups and workshops, connects adults who have ADHD with ADDA ambassadors, and maintains a directory of ADHD professionals.

ADHD Awareness Month
ADHDAwarenessMonth.org
Held each October, ADHD Awareness Month brings together mental health groups and government agencies for a mission: to educate the broader community about ADHD, reduce ADHD stigma, and celebrate positive aspects of ADHD.

Children and Adults with Attention-Deficit/Hyperactivity Disorder (CHADD)
CHADD.org
CHADD supports children and adults with ADHD through education and advocacy. CHADD maintains a directory of healthcare professionals specializing in ADHD.

Publications

ADDitude
AdditudeMag.com
ADDitude is the leading media network for those living with ADHD and the people who care for them. Their products include an online and print magazine, newsletters, webinars, e-books, and a professional directory.

ADHD: Parents Medication Guide
Psychiatry.org/File%20Library/Psychiatrists/Practice/Professional-Topics/Child-Adolescent-Psychiatry/adhd-parents-medication-guide.pdf
This medication guide is geared toward parents of children with ADHD, but it can be a very helpful guide for adults with ADHD, too.

Books

Mindfulness Meditations for ADHD: Improve Focus, Strengthen Self-Awareness, and Live More Fully by Merriam Sarcia Saunders, LMFT

Thriving with Adult ADHD: Skills to Strengthen Executive Functioning by Phil Boissiere, MFT

Succeeding With Adult ADHD: Daily Strategies to Help You Achieve Your Goals and Manage Your Life by Abigail Levrini, PhD, and Frances Prevatt, PhD

When an Adult You Love Has ADHD: Professional Advice for Parents, Partners, and Siblings by Russell A. Barkley, PhD

Federal Resources

Centers for Disease Control and Prevention (CDC)
CDC.gov/ncbddd/adhd/index.html
The CDC's ADHD page includes basics about ADHD, as well as statistical gems through FastStats (CDC.gov/nchs/fastats/adhd.htm).

Medline Plus
MedlinePlus.gov/attentiondeficithyperactivitydisorder.html
Medline Plus includes links on ADHD symptoms, diagnosis and tests, treatments and therapies and lifestyle changes.

National Institute of Mental Health (NIMH)
NIMH.NIH.gov/health/topics/attention-deficit-hyperactivity-disorder-adhd
The NIMH's ADHD page includes signs and symptoms, risk factors, and treatment and therapies. It also links to research studies and publications.

Therapist Resources

Good Therapy: GoodTherapy.org
Open Counseling: OpenCounseling.com
Psychology Today: PsychologyToday.com

Apps

Ten Percent Happier: mindfulness meditation courses
Headspace: mindfulness and guided meditations
Glo: online yoga and more
UCLA Mindful: mindfulness meditation courses

REFERENCES

ABC News. "Lisa Ling Reveals Surprise Diagnosis of ADD at age 40." June 16, 2014. ABCNews.go.com/blogs/entertainment/2014/06/lisa-ling-reveals-surprise -diagnosis-of-add-at-age-40.

ADA.gov. "A Guide to Disability Rights Laws." US Department of Justice, February 2020. ADA.gov/cguide.htm#anchor62335.

American Psychiatric Association. *Diagnostic and Statistical Manual of Mental Disorders (DSM-5)*. 5th ed. Arlington, VA: American Psychiatric Association, 2013.

Antoniou, Evangelia, Nikolaos Rigas, Eirini Orovou, Alexandros Papatrechas, and Angeliki Sarella. "ADHD Symptoms in Females of Childhood, Adolescent, Reproductive and Menopause Period." *Materia Socio-Medica* 33, no. 2 (June 2021): 114–8. doi: 10.5455/msm.2021.33.114-118.

Armstrong, Thomas. *The Power of Neurodiversity: Unleashing the Advantages of Your Differently Wired Brain*. Cambridge, MA: Da Capo Lifelong/Perseus Books, 2011.

Arns, Martijn, C. Richard Clark, Mark Trullinger, Roger deBeus, Martha Mack, and Michelle Aniftos. "Neurofeedback and Attention-Deficit/Hyperactivity-Disorder (ADHD) in Children: Rating the Evidence and Proposed Guidelines." *Applied Psychophysiology and Biofeedback* 45 (2020): 39–48. doi: 10.1007/s10484 -020-09455-2.

Barkley, Russell A., and Mariellen Fischer. "The Unique Contribution of Emotional Impulsiveness to Impairment in Major Life Activities in Hyperactive Children as Adults." *Journal of the American Academy of Child and Adolescent Psychiatry* 49, no. 5 (May 2010): 503–13. doi: 10.1097/00004583-201005000-00011.

Becerra-Culqui, Tracy A., Yuan, Rebecca Nash, Lee Cromwell, W. Dana Flanders, Darios Getahun, et al. "Mental Health of Transgender and Gender Nonconforming Youth Compared with Their Peers." *Pediatrics* 141, no. 5 (May 2018):e20173845. doi: 10.1542/peds.2017-3845.

Breda, V., L. A. Rohde, A. M. B. Menezes, L. Anselmi, A. Caye, et al. "Revisiting ADHD Age-of-Onset in Adults: To What Extent Should We Rely on the Recall of Childhood Symptoms?" *Psychological Medicine* 50, no. 5 (April 2020): 857–66. doi: 10.1017/S003329171900076X.

Carrer, Luiz Rogério Jorgensen Carrer. "Music and Sound in Time Processing of Children with ADHD." *Frontiers in Psychiatry* 28, no. 6 (September 2015): 127. doi: 10.3389/fpsyt.2015.00127.

Centers for Disease Control and Prevention. "Facts about ADHD." Last reviewed September 23, 2021. CDC.gov/ncbddd/adhd/data.html.

CHADD. "Asking for Workplace Accommodations." April 18, 2019. CHADD.org /adhd-weekly/asking-for-workplace-accommodations.

————. "Workplace Accommodations Can Make You and Your Employer Successful." February 23, 2017. CHADD.org/adhd-weekly/workplace-accommodations-can -make-you-and-your-employer-successful.

Cleveland Clinic. "Put the Phone Away! 3 Reasons Why Looking at It Before Bed Is a Bad Habit." April 22, 2019. Health.ClevelandClinic.org/put-the-phone-away -3-reasons-why-looking-at-it-before-bed-is-a-bad-habit.

Combs, Martha A., Will H. Canu, Joshua J. Broman-Fulks, et al. "Perceived Stress and ADHD Symptoms in Adults." *Journal of Attention Disorders* 19, no. 5 (May 2015): 425–34. doi: 10.1177/1087054712459558.

Cortese, Samuele, and David Coghill. "Twenty Years of Research on Attention-Deficit /Hyperactivity Disorder (ADHD): Looking Back, Looking Forward." *Evidence-Based Mental Health* 21, no. 4 (November 2018): 173–6. doi: 10.1136/ebmental -2018-300050.

Crawford, Aimee. "Bravo, Simone Biles, for Taking a Stand against ADHD Stigma." ESPN.com. September 21, 2010. ESPN.com/espnw/voices/story/_/id/17602540 /bravo-simone-biles-taking-stand-adhd-stigma.

Cross, Rob, and Andrew Parker. *The Hidden Power of Social Networks: Understanding How Work Really Gets Done in Organizations.* Boston: Harvard Business School Press, 2004.

Cross, Rob, Peter H. Gray, Alexandra Gerbasi, and Dimitris Assimakopoulos. "Building Engagement from the Ground Up: How Top Organizations Leverage Networks to Drive Employee Engagement." *Organizational Dynamics* 41, no. 3 (July 2012): 202–11. doi:10.1016/j.orgdyn.2012.03.004.

Cross, Rob, Wayne E. Baker, and Andrew Parker. "What Creates Energy in Organizations?" *MIT Sloan Management Review* 44, no. 4 (Summer 2003): 51–6.

Cuncic, Arlin. "Why Gen Z Is More Open to Talking about Their Mental Health." *Verywell Mind*. Updated March 25, 2021. VerywellMind.com/why-gen-z-is-more-open-to -talking-about-their-mental-health-5104730.

Danielson, Melissa L., Rebecca H. Bitsko, Reem M. Ghandour, Joseph R. Holbrook, Michael D. Kogan, and Stephen J. Blumberg. "Prevalence of Parent-Reported ADHD Diagnosis and Associated Treatment among U.S. Children and Adolescents, 2016." *Journal of Clinical Child and Adolescent Psychology* 47, no. 2 (March–April 2018): 199–212.

Dawson, Anne E., Brian T. Wymbs, Christine A. Gidycz, Michelle Pride, and Wilson Figueroa (2017) "Exploring Rates of Transgender Individuals and Mental Health Concerns in an Online Sample." *International Journal of Transgenderism* 18, no. 3 (April 2017): 295–304, doi: 10.1080/15532739.2017.1314797.

del Campo, Natalia, Samuel R. Chamberlain, Barbara J. Sahakian, and Trevor W. Robbins. "The Roles of Dopamine and Noradrenaline in the Pathophysiology and Treatment of Attention-Deficit/Hyperactivity Disorder." *Biological Psychiatry* 69, no. 12 (June 2011): e145–57. doi:10.1016/j.biopsych.2011.02.036.

den Houting, Jacquiline. "Neurodiversity: An Insider's Perspective." *Autism* 23, no. 2 (February 2019): 271–3. doi: 10.1177/1362361318820762.

Dorani, Farangis, Denise Bijlenga, Aartjan T. F. Beekman, Eus J. W. van Someren, and J. J. Sandra Kooij. "Prevalence of Hormone-related Mood Disorder Symptoms in Women with ADHD." *Journal of Psychiatric Research* 133 (January 2021): 10–5. doi: 10.1016/j.jpsychires.2020.12.005.

Doyle, Nancy. "Neurodiversity at Work: A Biopsychosocial Model and the Impact on Working Adults." *British Medical Bulletin* 135, no. 2 (October 2020): 108–25. doi: 10.1093/bmb/ldaa021.

Eddy, Laura D., Heather A. Jones, Daniel Snipes, Nicole Karjane, and Dace Svikis. "Associations between ADHD Symptoms and Occupational, Interpersonal, and Daily Life Impairments among Pregnant Women." *Journal of Attention Disorders* 23, no. 9 (July 2019): 976–84. doi: 10.1177/1087054716685839.

Faraone, Stephen V., and Henrik Larsson. "Genetics of Attention Deficit Hyperactivity Disorder." *Molecular Psychiatry* 24 (April 2019): 562–75. doi: 10.1038/s41380 -018-0070-0.

Gillespie-Lynch, Kristen, Nidal Daou, Rita Obeid, Siobhan Reardon, Spogmay Khan, and Emily J. Goldknopf. "What Contributes to Stigma Towards Autistic University Students and Students with Other Diagnoses?" *Journal of Autism and Developmental Disorders* 51, no. 2 (February 2021): 459–75. doi: 10.1007/s10803-020-04556-7.

Gilman, Lois. "How to Succeed in Business with ADHD." *ADDitude*. Updated February 18, 2021. ADDitudeMag.com/adhd-entrepreneur-stories-jetblue-kinkos -jupitermedia.

Heasman, Brett, and Alex Gillespie. "Neurodivergent Intersubjectivity: Distinctive Features of How Autistic People Create Shared Understanding." *Autism* 23, no. 4 (May 2019): 910–21. doi: 10.1177/1362361318785172.

Hirsch, Oliver, Mira Lynn Chavanon, and Hanna Christiansen. "Emotional Dysregulation Subgroups in Patients with Adult Attention-Deficit/Hyperactivity Disorder (ADHD): A Cluster Analytic Approach." *Scientific Reports* 9 (2019): 5639. doi: 10.1038 /s41598-019-42018-y.

Hisler, Garrett, Jean M. Twenge, and Zlatan Krizan. "Associations between Screen Time and Short Sleep Duration among Adolescents Varies by Media Type: Evidence from a Cohort Study." *Sleep Medicine* 66 (2020): 92–102. doi: 10.1016 /j.sleep.2019.08.007.

Hoogman, Martino, Janita Bralten, Derrek P. Hibar, Maarten Mennes, Marcel P. Zwiers, Lizanne S. J. Schweren, Kimm J. E. van Hulzen, Sarah E. Medland, et al. "Subcortical Brain Volume Differences in Participants with Attention Deficit Hyperactivity Disorder in Children and Adults: A Cross-sectional Mega-Analysis." *Lancet Psychiatry* 4, no. 4 (April 2017): 310–9. doi:10.1016/S2215-0366(17)30049-4.

Kapp, Steven K., Kristen Gillespie-Lynch, Lauren E. Sherman, and Ted Hutman. "Deficit, Difference, or Both? Autism and Neurodiversity." *Developmental Psychology* 49, no. 1 (January 2013): 59–71. doi: 10.1037/a0028353.

Katzman, Martin A., Timothy S. Bilkey, Pratap R. Chokka, Angelo Fallu, and Larry J. Klassen. "Adult ADHD and Comorbid Disorders: Clinical Implications of a Dimensional Approach". *BMC Psychiatry* 17, no. 1 (August 22, 2017): 302. doi: 10.1186 /s12888-017-1463-3.

Kessler, Ronald C., Lenard Adler, Russell Barkley, Joseph Biederman, C. Keith Conners, Olga Demler, Stephen V. Faraone, Laurence L. Greenhill, et al. "The Prevalence and Correlates of Adult ADHD in the United States: Results from the National Comorbidity Survey Replication." *American Journal of Psychiatry* 163, no. 4 (April 2006): 716–23. doi: 10.1176/ajp.2006.163.4.716.

Kim, Boong-Nyun, Jae-Won Kim, Hyejin Kang, Soo-Churl Cho, Min-Sup Shin, Hee-Jeong Yoo, Soon-Beom Hong, and Dong Soo Lee. "Regional Differences in Cerebral Perfusion Associated with the Alpha-2A-adrenergic Receptor Genotypes in Attention Deficit Hyperactivity Disorder." *Journal of Psychiatry and Neuroscience* 35, no. 5 (September 2010): 330–6. doi:10.1503/jpn.090168.

Kolding, Line, Vera Ehrenstein, Lars Pedersen, Puk Sandager, Olav B. Petersen, Niels Uldbjerg, and Lars H. Pedersen. "Associations between ADHD Medication Use in Pregnancy and Severe Malformations Based on Prenatal and Postnatal Diagnoses: A Danish Registry-Based Study." *Journal of Clinical Psychiatry* 82, no. 1 (January 2021): 20m13458. doi: 10.4088/JCP.20m13458.

Kooij, J. J. S., D. Bijlenga, L. Salerno, R. Jaeschke, I Bitter, J. Balázs, J. Thome, G. Dom, S. Kasper, et al. "Updated European Consensus Statement on Diagnosis and Treatment of Adult ADHD." *European Psychiatry* 56 (February 2019): 14–34. doi: 10.1016/j.eurpsy.2018.11.001.

Koren, Gideon, Yael Barer, and Asher Ornoy. "Fetal Safety of Methylphenidate—A Scoping Review and Meta Analysis." *Reproductive Toxicology* 93 (April 2020): 230–34. doi: 10.1016/j.reprotox.2020.03.003.

Louden, Kathleen. "Gender Identity Issues Related to Autism, ADHD." *Medscape.* March 17, 2014. Medscape.com/viewarticle/822077.

Luman, Marjolein, Alky Papanikolau, and Jaap Oosterlaan. "The Unique and Combined Effects of Reinforcement and Methylphenidate on Temporal Information Processing in Attention-Deficit/Hyperactivity Disorder." *Journal of Clinical Psychopharmacology* 35, no. 4 (August 2015): 414–21. doi: 10.1097/JCP.0000000000000349.

Mahdi, Soheil, Marisa Viljoen, Rafael Massuti, Melissa Selb, Omar Almodayfer, Sunil Karande, Petrus J. de Vries, et al. "An International Qualitative Study of Ability and Disability in ADHD Using the WHO-ICF Framework." *European Child and Adolescent Psychiatry* 26, no. 10 (October 2017): 1219–31. doi: 10.1007/s00787-017-0983-1.

Mazaheri, Ali, Sharon Coffey-Corina, George R. Mangun, Evelijne M. Bekker, Anne S. Berry, and Blythe A. Corbett. "Functional Disconnection of Frontal Cortex and Visual Cortex in Attention-Deficit/Hyperactivity Disorder." *Biological Psychiatry* 67, no. 7 (April 1, 2010): 617–23. doi:10.1016/j.biopsych.2009.11.022.

McRae, Kateri, and James J. Gross. "Emotion Regulation." *Emotion* 20, no. 1 (February 2020): 1–9. doi: 10.1037/emo0000703.

Mehren, Aylin, Markus Reichert, David Coghill, Helge H. O. Müller, Niclas Braun, and Alexandra Philipsen. "Physical Exercise in Attention Deficit Hyperactivity Disorder—Evidence and Implications for the Treatment of Borderline Personality Disorder." *Borderline Personality Disorder and Emotion Dysregulation* 7, no. 1 (2020). doi: 10.1186/s40479-019-0115-2.

Miranda, Monica Carolina, Thais Barbosa, Mauro Muszkat, Camila Cruz Rodrigues, Elaine Girão Sinnes, Luzia Flavia S. Coelho, et al. (2012) "Performance Patterns in Conners' CPT among Children with Attention Deficit Hyperactivity Disorder and Dyslexia." *Arquivos de Neuro-Psiquiatria* 70, no. 2 (February 2012): 91–96. doi: 10.1590/s0004-282x2012000200004.

Murphy, P., and R. Schachar. "Use of Self-ratings in the Assessment of Symptoms of Attention Deficit Hyperactivity Disorder in Adults." *American Journal of Psychiatry* 157, no. 7 (July 2000): 1156–9. doi: 10.1176/appi.ajp.157.7.1156.

Nazari, Mohammad A., Mohammad M. Miroo, Mazaher Rezaei, and Mojtaba Soltanlou. "Emotional Stimuli Facilitate Time Perception in Children with Attention-Deficit/Hyperactivity Disorder." *Journal of Neuropsychology* 12, no. 2 (June 2018): 165–75. doi:10.1111/jnp.12111.

Newnham, Nicole, and Lebrecht, James, dirs. *Crip Camp: A Disability Revolution*. Los Gatos, CA: Netflix, 2020.

Nøvik, Torunn Stene, Amaia Hervas, Stephen J. Ralston, Søren Dalsgaard, Rob Rodrigues Pereira, Maria J. Lorenzo, and ADORE Study Group. "Influence of Gender on Attention-Deficit/Hyperactivity Disorder in Europe—ADORE."

European Child and Adolescent Psychiatry Suppl. 1 (December 2006): 1–24. doi: 10.1007/s00787-006-1003-z.

Oliver, Michael. *Understanding Disability: From Theory to Practice*. New York: Palgrave Macmillan, 1996.

Oller, D. Kimbrough. "Evolutionary-developmental Modeling of Neurodiversity and Psychopathology." *Behavioral and Brain Sciences*. 42 (2019): e19. doi: 10.1017 /S0140525X18001103.

Perry, Patrick. "ADHD: Living in Overdrive" *Saturday Evening Post*. October 17, 2012. SaturdayEveningPost.com/2012/10/adhd/3.

Ptacek, Radek, Simon Weissenberger, Ellen Braaten, Martina Klicperova-Baker, Michal Goetz, Jiri Raboch, Martina Vnukova, and George B. Stefano. "Clinical Implications of the Perception of Time in Attention Deficit Hyperactivity Disorder (ADHD): A Review." *Medical Science Monitor* 25 (2019): 3918–24. doi: 10.12659 /MSM.914225.

Quinn, Patricia O., and Manisha Madhoo. "A Review of Attention-Deficit/Hyperactivity Disorder in Women and Girls: Uncovering This Hidden Diagnosis." *Primary Care Companion for CNS Disorders* 16, no. 3 (2014): PCC.13r01596. doi:10.4088 /PCC.13r01596.

Ríos-Hernández, Alejandra, José A. Alda, Andreu Farran-Codina, Estrella Ferreira-García, and Maria Izquierdo-Pulido. "The Mediterranean Diet and ADHD in Children and Adolescents." *Pediatrics* 139, no. 2 (February 2017): e20162027. doi: 10.1542/peds.2016-2027.

Robberecht, Harry, Annelies A. J. Verlaet, Annelies Breynaert, Tess De Bruyne, and Nina Hermans. "Magnesium, Iron, Zinc, Copper and Selenium Status in Attention-Deficit/Hyperactivity Disorder (ADHD)." *Molecules* 25, no. 19 (2020): 4440. doi: 10.3390/molecules25194440.

Rodden, Janice. "Having ADHD and Taking Medicine for It Is Nothing to Be Ashamed Of." *ADDitude*. Updated April 30, 2021. ADDitudeMag.com/simone-biles-adhd -olympic-gymnast-publicly-addresses-condition.

Rucklidge, Julia J. "Gender Differences in Attention-Deficit/Hyperactivity Disorder." *Psychiatric Clinics of North America* 33, no. 2 (June 2010): 357–73. doi: 10.1016 /j.psc.2010.01.006.

Ryan, R. M., and E. L. Deci. "Self-determination Theory and the Facilitation of Intrinsic Motivation, Social Development, and Well-being." *American Psychologist* 55, no. 1 (January 2000): 68–78. doi: 10.1037//0003-066x.55.1.68.

Sedgwick, Jane Ann, Andrew Merwood, and Philip Asherson. "The Positive Aspects of Attention Deficit Hyperactivity Disorder: A Qualitative Investigation of Successful Adults with ADHD." *Attention Deficit and Hyperactivity Disorders* 11, no. 3 (September 2019): 241–53. doi: 10.1007/s12402-018-0277-6.

Shaw, Philip, Argyris Stringaris, Joel Nigg, and Ellen Leibenluft. "Emotion Dysregulation in Attention Deficit Hyperactivity Disorder." *American Journal of Psychiatry* 171, no. 3 (March 2014): 276–93. doi: 10.1176/appi.ajp.2013.13070966.

Sherman, Carl. "Is ADHD a Disability? Your Legal Rights at Work." *ADDitude.* February 7, 2021. ADDitudeMag.com/workplace-legal-protection.

Silberman, Steve. *NeuroTribes: The Legacy of Autism and the Future of Neurodiversity.* New York: Avery, 2015.

Simon, Viktória, Pál Czobor, Sára Bálint, Agnes Mészáros, and István Bitter. "Prevalence and Correlates of Adult Attention-Deficit Hyperactivity Disorder: Meta-Analysis." *British Journal of Psychiatry* 194, no. 3 (March 2009): 204–11. doi: 10.1192/bjp.bp.107.048827.

Singer, Judy. *NeuroDiversity: The Birth of an Idea.* Self-published, Amazon Digital Services, 2017. Kindle.

_____. "Odd People In: The Birth of Community Amongst People on the Autism Spectrum: A Personal Exploration of a New Social Movement Based on Neurological Diversity." An honors thesis presented to the Faculty of Humanities and Social Science, the University of Technology, Sydney, 1998.

_____. "Why Can't You Be Normal for Once in Your Life?: From a 'Problem with No Name' to a New Category of Disability." In *Disability Discourse,* edited by M. Corker and S. French. Buckingham: Open University Press, 1999.

Smith, Anna, Eric Taylor, Jody Warner Rogers, Stuart Newman, and Katya Rubia. "Evidence for a Pure Time Perception Deficit in Children with ADHD." *Journal of Child Psychology and Psychiatry* 43, no. 4 (May 2002): 529–42. doi: 10.1111/1469-7610.00043.

Smith, Joanna E., Janet Richardson, Caroline Hoffman, and Karen Pilkington. "Mindful-ness-Based Stress Reduction as Supportive Therapy in Cancer Care: Systematic Review." *Journal of Advanced Nursing* 52, no. 3 (November 2005): 315–27. doi: 10.1111/j.1365-2648.2005.03592.x.

Sobanski, Esther, Tobias Banaschewski, Philip Asherson, Jan Buitelaar, Wai Chen, Barbara Franke, Martin Holtmann, Bertram Krumm, et al. "Emotional Lability in Children and Adolescents with Attention Deficit/Hyperactivity Disorder (ADHD): Clinical Correlates and Familial Prevalence." *Journal of Child Psychology and Psychiatry* 51, no. 8 (August 2010): 915–23. doi: 10.1111/j.1469-7610.2010.02217.x.

Sonuga-Barke, Edmund, and Anita Thapar. "The Neurodiversity Concept: Is It Helpful for Clinicians and Scientists?" *Lancet Psychiatry* 8, no. 7 (July 2021): 559–61. doi: 10.1016/S2215-0366(21)00167-X.

Sörös, Peter, Eliza Hoxhaj, Patricia Borel, Chiharu Sadohara, Bernd Feige, Swantje Matthies, et al. "Hyperactivity/Restlessness Is Associated with Increased Functional Connectivity in Adults with ADHD: A Dimensional Analysis of Resting State fMRI." *BMC Psychiatry* 19, no. 1 (January 2019): 43. doi:10.1186/s12888-019-2031-9.

Surman, Craig B. H., Joseph Biederman, Thomas Spencer, Carolyn A. Millder, Katie M. McDermott, and Stephen V. Faraone. "Understanding Deficient Emotional Self-Regulation in Adults with Attention Deficit Hyperactivity Disorder: A Controlled Study." *Attention Deficit and Hyperactivity Disorders* 5, no. 3 (September 2013): 273–81. doi: 10.1007/s12402-012-0100-8.

Tannen, Deborah. *Conversational Style: Analyzing Talk among Friends.* New York: Oxford University Press, 1984.

Thapar, Anita, Miriam Cooper, Olga Eyre, and Kate Langley. "What Have We Learnt about the Causes of ADHD?" *Journal of Child Psychology and Psychiatry* 54, no. 1 (January 2013): 3–16. doi: 10.1111/j.1469-7610.2012.02611.x.

Tripp, Gail, and Jeffery R. Wickens. "Neurobiology of ADHD." *Neuropharmacology* 57, no. 7–8 (December 2009): 579–89. doi: 10.1016/j.neuropharm.2009.07.026.

Ustun, Berk, Lenard A. Adler, Cynthia Rudin, Stephen V. Faraone, Thomas J. Spencer, Patricia Berglund, Michael J. Gruber, and Ronald C. Kessler. "The World Health Organization Adult Attention-Deficit/Hyperactivity Disorder Self-Report Screening Scale for *DSM-5*." *JAMA Psychiatry* 74, no. 5 (2017): 520–26. doi:10.1001/jamapsychiatry.2017.0298.

Vaillant, George E. *Triumphs of Experience: The Men of the Harvard Grant Study.* Cambridge, MA: Harvard University Press, 2012.

Vohs, Kathleen D., Roy F. Baumeister, Brandon J. Schmeichel, Jean M. Twenge, Noelle M. Nelson, and Dianne M. Tice. "Making Choices Impairs Subsequent Self-Control: A Limited-Resource Account of Decision Making, Self-Regulation, and Active Initiative." *Journal of Personality and Social Psychology* 94, no. 5 (May 2008): 883–98. doi: 10.1037/0022-3514.94.5.883.

Von Culin, Katherine R., Eli Tsukayama, and Angela L. Duckworth "Unpacking Grit: Motivational Correlates of Perseverance and Passion for Long-Term Goals." *Journal of Positive Psychology* 9, no. 4 (2014): 306–12. doi: 10.1080/17439760 .2014.898320.

Walg, Marco, Johannes Oepen, and Helmut Prior. "Adjustment of Time Perception in the Range of Seconds and Milliseconds: The Nature of Time-Processing Alterations in Children with ADHD." *Journal of Attention Disorders* 19, no. 9 (September 2015): 755–63. doi: 10.1177/1087054712454570.

Wansink, Brian, and Jeffery Sobal. "Mindless Eating: The 200 Daily Food Decisions We Overlook." *Environment and Behavior* 39, no. 1 (January 2007): 106–23. doi:10.1177/0013916506295573.

White, Holly A., and Priti Shah. "Uninhibited Imaginations: Creativity in Adults with Attention-Deficit/Hyperactivity Disorder." *Personality and Individual Differences* 40, no. 6 (April 2006): 1121–31. doi: 10.1016/j.paid.2005.11.007.

White, Holly A., and Priti Shah. "Creative Style and Achievement in Adults with Attention-Deficit/Hyperactivity Disorder." *Personality and Individual Differences* 50, no. 5 (April 2011): 673–7. doi: 10.1016/j.paid.2010.12.015.

Young, Susan, Nicoletta Adamo, Bryndís Björk Ásgeirsdóttir, Polly Breanney, Michelle Beckett, William Colley, Sally Cubbin, et al. "Females with ADHD: An Expert Consensus Statement Taking a Lifespan Approach Providing Guidance for the Identification and Treatment of Attention-Deficit/Hyperactivity Disorder in Girls and Women." *BMC Psychiatry* 20, no. 1 (August 2020): 404. doi: 10.1186 /s12888-020-02707-9.

INDEX